How to be BETTER at PRESENTING

In Person and Online

Mike Grocott

Copyright © 2020 Mike Grocott

All rights reserved.

No portion of this book may be reproduced, stored in a retrieval system or transmitted in any form or means (including electronic, mechanical, photocopy, recording, scanning or other) without prior permission from the copyright holder, except for brief quotations in critical reviews or articles.

ISBN: 9798558287868

Cover design by Dave Brogden.

Acknowledgements

Particular thanks need to go to Clare, Dom, Roger, Charlie, Michael, Darren, Liz and Emee for their time, input and encouragement whilst I was writing this book.

I have singular thanks for David Hyner without whose guidance, support and accountability this book would not exist. The contacts that I have met through being part of David's Mastermind Group have also proved to be fountains of knowledge and wisdom in helping me to write this book.

I also need to thank those people who have agreed to allow me to include them, or their words, as examples in this book. You'll meet them as you go through…

And finally, a thank you to the many hundreds of people who have attended my courses and/or asked me to work with them as a coach. They have helped me to create, hone and improve these frameworks over time to be the frameworks that they are today. So thank you to all those people who, at one time or another, have let me practise on them!

Contents

About this Book 1

Part 1 5
    Where Confidence Comes From 7
    The Confidence Formula 11

Part 2 13
    How to Create Great Content 15
    The YAT Triangle 17
    When Larry Met Ali 27
    The PRESENTER Framework 29
    The Content Pie Sandwich 45
    The ABC for Short Videos 65

Part 3 67
    How to Deliver with Confidence 69
    The Confidence Cycle 71
    The SPEAKER Framework 73
    Be Environmentally Aware 93
    Don't Hope, Do! 97

Further Information 99
    The *"Interact better. Achieve more."* Series 101
    About the Author 103

About this Book

I'm curious.

Why are you reading this? What is it about the subject of presentations that makes you want to read a book about getting better at presenting?

Perhaps you are like Mary, Matt, Daniel, Charlene or Richard.

Mary
Mary is the Compliance Director for a hugely successful IT company. She has decades of experience and is the company's subject matter expert in this area. Every year she has to do a 15-minute presentation at the "Company Day" event. All 400 of the employees will be in the audience.

Mary absolutely dreads doing it!

Just the thought of standing up in front of everyone and giving a presentation scares her witless and makes her anxious for days and days before the event.

Matt
Matt set up his video production company straight out of University. He is talented, driven and ambitious and has high goals for his company. He doesn't want to fail.

Matt recognises that if his business is going to be a success he will need to present to many people, at all levels of organisations. The snag is that he has not done much presenting before and is conscious that if he doesn't do it well, he will not create the positive impression for himself and his company that he needs to and he might not actually achieve his goals.

Daniel
A recognised expert in his field, Daniel has helped many business owners to sell their companies, sometimes for millions of pounds. Business owners come to him because of his reputation – he knows what he's doing!

But whenever he stands up in front of an audience to tell them what he does, it never quite comes out right. It never seems to come out in a way that his audience can understand or remember and this both flusters and frustrates Daniel, in equal measure.

He's great at what he does but rubbish at telling other people!

Charlene
Charlene is a professional speaker, a great professional speaker in fact. Her presentations are entertaining, thought-provoking and life-changing.

But she wants to be better. Charlene wants to take her presentations to the next level, to be *the* person that people think of when they need a speaker in her niche of Mind Management..

Richard
Richard owns Stone Junction, a successful, award-winning PR agency, based in Stafford. His firm gets asked to tender for numerous opportunities but their conversion rate is not as high as Richard would like it to be. Richard believes that it's something to do with the sales presentations that they are making to their prospective clients.

Richard has a great team, a very knowledgeable and capable team, but somehow this is not coming across well enough to the outside world.

Do those stories sound familiar or resonate with you? I wouldn't be surprised if they did!

In fact Mary, Matt, Daniel, Charlene and Richard are all real people, people with whom I've had the pleasure of working over a number of years, people who have become better, more confident presenters and achieved what they wanted to achieve:

Mary
Mary actually enjoyed her presentation at the Company Day. She even had the confidence to interview one of her colleagues up on the stage with her as part of her presentation. The run-up to the event was not its normal anxiety-fest either.

Her colleagues noticed the difference in her presentation as well (and told her so too).

Matt
Matt is now an engaging, charismatic and successful speaker. He has delivered numerous presentations to people at all levels of business. He has successfully grown his business to be one of the top 50 production companies in the UK.

Daniel
Daniel has a clear plan for telling people what he does and is looking forward to an effective, fluster-free, non-frustrating experience the next time he presents.

Charlene
Charlene is going from strength to strength, gathering recognition and reputation as a go-to speaker and thought-leader on Mind Management. Her presentations are keenly focussed on her audience and what she can do to help them.

Richard
In less than four years, Richard's business has trebled in size. He believes that a key factor in this incredible growth was his team becoming better, more confident presenters.

I'm happy, chuffed and proud to have played a small part in all of these achievements, although I totally recognise that they did the hard yards!

So what did we do? How were these achievements accomplished?

In essence, by using what's in this book!

In this book you will find a collection of guides, ideas and frameworks to help you to be a better, more confident presenter. (I'll collectively refer to them as "frameworks" from now on for simplicity).

I've created, refined and used these frameworks over many years to become what they are today. Their goal is to be simple enough to be remembered, easy enough to be put into practice and robust enough to actually be of some use in the first place!

So this book is about practicality. It's about helping you to understand the purpose of the frameworks and how you can then put them into practice, so you can become a better, more confident presenter and achieve your goals and aspirations.

This is therefore, in effect, a self-help book.

To get the most out of this book I would suggest that you first read this book from front to back as that represents the logical and chronological approach that you would take to creating and delivering a presentation.

Once you've done that you can dip in and out of the book as required as the frameworks are essentially standalone in nature focusing on particular aspects of presenting. That being said, the different frameworks are interrelated and do cross-reference each other on occasion.

Due to the circular nature of the cross-references, sometimes I'll mention something in passing that I will cover later in detail in the book. For clarity, I'll highlight those occurrences with an arrow and highlight to which future section the reference applies.

There are also some other callouts that are highlighted in this book:

This book can also be used as a workbook, to help you as you go through the process of creating your own presentations. I've created a number of resources that are available from the Resources section of my website: www.intercog.co.uk.

To supplement the content in this book, I have also created some video content. (It's sometimes easier to show you than tell you). These video resources are also available from the Resources section of my website: www.intercog.co.uk.

People that know me well would tell you that I like a good tangent and so you'll find a few of these tangents as you go through the book. They are not core to the book but will add some personal asides, notes and references that are relevant at that point.

Online Considerations

The frameworks presented in this book are equally applicable to presenting in person and presenting online, whether that be a "live" presentation over the Internet or a recorded presentation that is viewed later. (I'll use the term "online" in this book to refer to either format)

I will therefore include an "Online Considerations" section at the end of each framework to cover any differences and additional thoughts that relate to presenting online.

So let's start with a quick look at where confidence comes from...

Part 1

Where Confidence Comes From

Which came first: the chicken or the egg?

It's a well-known conundrum to which there is, of course, no obvious answer.

And there is a similar potential dilemma when talking about presenting:

> Do you become a better presenter by being more confident?

> Or do you become more confident by being a better presenter?

There is probably some truth in both statements.

But does one actually come before the other or do we have another chicken and egg scenario here?

Fortunately, the answer is, we don't!

Being a better presenter comes first.

Or, more accurately, knowing *how* to be a better presenter comes first.

If you know how to be a better presenter then when you put that knowledge into practice and present you will *be* a better presenter. If you are better when you present, then your presentations will be more effective and more successful. That will give you more confidence for your next presentation which will in turn make you an even better presenter.

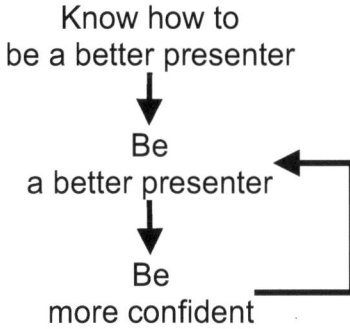

So there is a cyclical aspect to this but there is a clear place to start: know *how* to be a better presenter.

And this book will show you *how* to be a better presenter so you can *be* a better presenter and therefore more confident when presenting.

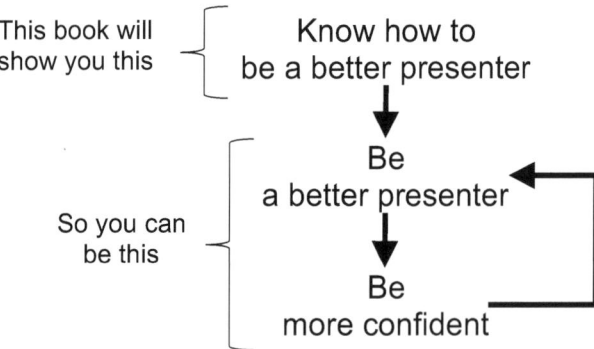

And by being a better, more confident presenter it will help you to achieve what you want, whatever that may be.

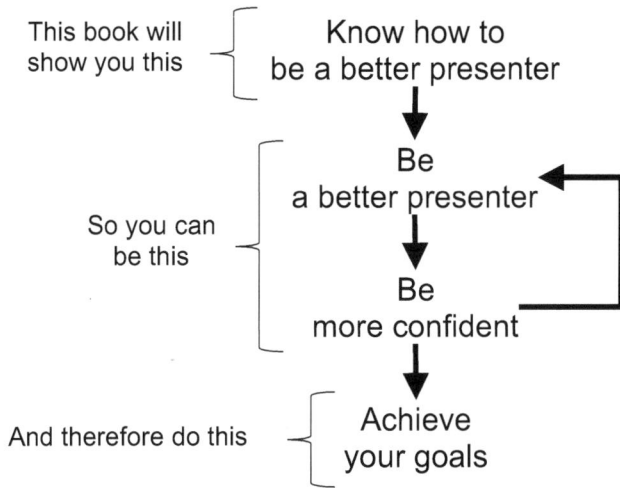

An interesting observation here is that for many people, they see being more confident as a goal in and of itself. It's something that they are aiming to achieve and that's absolutely fine and a perfectly valid goal.

However, for those people that see increased confidence as a goal, I would ask them this: "So what will that increased confidence bring you?", "What difference will it make to you?".

Is it less stress, more enjoyment, better results, making it easier to just get the presentation over and done with or even simply a good night's sleep the night before?

These are all possible outcomes that will come from being more confident. They are clearly goals, though, that people are wanting to achieve. They are also more quantifiable than simply "being more confident".

So when you dig a bit deeper, although it might appear that increased confidence is a goal itself, it is also definitely still a means to achieve those other more tangible goals.

Whichever way you look at it, confidence is something that is built up over time. So let's have a look in more detail about what the building blocks of confidence actually are.

The Confidence Formula

For defining and understanding the building blocks of confidence.

The Confidence Formula is very simple:

$C = A + P + S$

That's the easy to remember mnemonic!

(I'll also refer to it in this book as the **CAPS** Framework.)

Expanding it into a slightly fuller format:

Confidence = **A**udience-focus + **P**reparation + **S**kills

In other words, how confident you are is the sum total of how much you consider your audience, how much preparation you do and how skilled you are at creating and delivering presentations.

The more you do with regard to each of these three aspects, the more confident you will be.

The less you do, the less confident you will be.

And if you ignore one aspect (or two), you won't be as confident as you could be.

It's a bit like a three-legged stool at a breakfast-bar in a kitchen:

- the legs need to be long enough for it to be useful as a stool when you sit next to the bar so you can eat your breakfast
- if the legs are not long enough, although you might be able to sit on your stool (it might be uncomfortable), you certainly wouldn't be able to reach your breakfast
- and if one leg or two legs are a lot shorter than the others, you won't be able to actually sit on it at all

The goal is therefore to have a stool (C) with long-enough legs of similar lengths (APS).

The frameworks in this book will therefore look at these three different aspects of the Confidence Formula and show you how to have a better focus on your audience, be better prepared and have better all-round presentation skills.

They are all about creating a taller more usable stool, as it were.

But before I move on to those frameworks though, I have a quick tangent for you on over-confidence. (You'll get used to my tangents!)

Over-confidence comes from a false belief or self-perception by a speaker that their audience-focus, preparation and/or skills are at a higher level than they actually are in reality. Over-confidence can also come from a lack of being bothered. Whatever the cause, speakers who are over-confident are less likely to be effective as a presenter and more likely to trip themselves up.

It is essential, therefore, to have an accurate, reflective and honest understanding of where you really are with regard to your audience-focus, preparation and skills.

After all, trying to sit on a stool that's not as big as you thought it was, never ends well...

Online Considerations

Taking an audience-focused approach is equally as important when delivering online as it is in person.

Much of your preparation will remain the same. There are, however, some differences to your preparation when you are considering online delivery and these are mainly in the realm of what you will need to help you to deliver the presentation.

*This is something I'll cover in more detail in the **PRESENTER** and **Be Environmentally Aware** Frameworks when I talk about the delivery aids that you will need.*

The vast majority of your in-person delivery skills are also going to be required when delivering online. Again, though, there are some different and additional skills that you need to deliver effectively online. These will generally complement your in-person delivery skills but in some cases will require you to act, and think, differently.

*This is something I'll cover in more detail in various places in the **SPEAKER** Framework.*

Part 2

How to Create Great Content

You've got a presentation to deliver and you need to create the content for that presentation.

So where do you start?

I normally ask this question of the people that I'm working with in a training or coaching capacity. If they reply "Well I open my laptop and start PowerPoint..." then I politely close their laptop and hit them over the head with it!

OK – so maybe I jokingly threaten to do that and we all laugh about the idea. (I've never actually hit anyone!)

But in reality, I'm very much not joking!

Starting with the slides is completely the wrong place to start. Even thinking about your slides at this point is a detrimental distraction.

There is a much better place to start and that's by thinking about your audience and about your message.

You can then create your content with one eye fixed firmly on your audience and the other on your message.

You can focus on how to make it *interesting*, so your audience will want to listen to you, *understandable*, so they will hear your message clearly and *memorable*, so they won't forget it.

So in this part of the book I've got five frameworks for you, frameworks that are tried, tested and proven to work, frameworks that together will help you to create great content.

The YAT Triangle

For considering the important relationships between you, your audience and what it is you're talking about.

Think audience first!

It's a phrase that I use so many times when I'm working with people. It's a philosophy that holds true for lots of things: presenting, networking, teamwork and many more. In fact, it's valid for any and every form of communication.

Taking a proactive approach and focussing on your audience first is the best way to start thinking about a presentation and the YAT Triangle will help you to do that.

In her book "How to be Brilliant at Public Speaking", Sarah Lloyd-Hughes talks about "Audience-focussed Preparation". Her thoughts on that resonated with my own experiences and helped me to refine the YAT Triangle into what it is today.

The YAT Triangle considers the relationships between:

- **Y**ou
- your **A**udience
- and the **T**opic about which you'll be talking

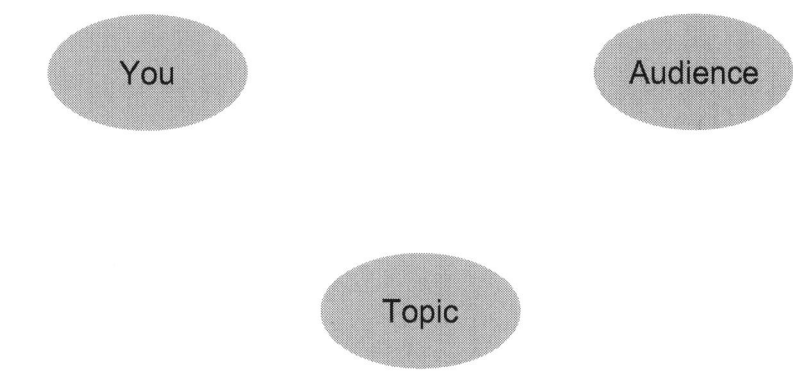

Let's have a look at each relationship in turn.

Your perspective on your audience

So what will your audience be like?

There are many questions that you could ask about them.

Some are factual ones, for example:

- How many people will be there?
- What companies/organisations/industries will they be from?
- At what levels within those companies/organisations are they?
- What roles do they have within those companies/organisations?

And some are about them as people, for example:

- Are they chatty or formal?
- Are they creative or logical?
- Are they young or old?
- Are they novices or experts?

There are many more and they will vary from presentation to presentation.

You also need to consider what you are expecting from them, for example:

- Are they just going to sit and listen?
- Will they want to ask questions?
- Are they going to try and give you a hard time?

And how well do you know them? Some people find it easier to talk to strangers than people they know and some people are the exact opposite. Either way, how well you know your audience will affect how you go about speaking to them.

Taking a moment to consider what you know about your audience right at the start of the presentation development process is massively important as the information gathered at that point will help you to focus your presentation on them and their needs as an audience.

In summary:

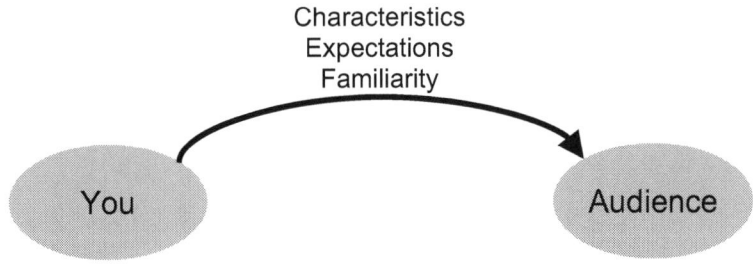

Your audience's perspective on you

Now let's look at it from the other direction.

What does your audience know about you? Perhaps nothing!

Perhaps just the basic information like your name, company and job title. Maybe they have heard you speak before. Or maybe they know you well!

And what's your reputation as a speaker?

What's your reputation for being experienced and knowledgeable in the area about which you will be speaking?

Will they assume things about you because of your job title, company or any letters you have put after your name?

All of these factors will set the audience's expectations for you and your presentation (as will the nature of the topic but more on that later).

So take some time to look at it from their perspective, to think about what they know about you and what their expectations are.

In summary:

Your audience's perspective on the topic

Interest and importance are two very different things!

Here's a simple example to show the difference. My company is VAT registered. Every quarter I need to submit a VAT return or I will get fined. It's therefore important to me to do this (as I don't want to lose money). However, I'll let you draw your own conclusions as to how interesting I find doing my tax return...

So with regard to your audience, it is important to recognise that some people will want to listen to you because the topic is important to them and some people will be in your audience because they find the topic interesting. Their motivations for being there could well be quite different.

*To be clear, I'm not talking here about making your presentation interesting - I'm talking about why your audience is there. Regardless of why they are there, your presentation needs to be interesting and I'll cover that later in the **PRESENTER** Framework.*

Also bear in mind that your potential audience might not have much information on what it is that you'll be talking about. Do they only have the title? Or do they have a precis as well? Or perhaps all they know is that it's you! Whatever information they have, whatever you provide, it needs to tick the boxes of importance and interest.

You also need to think about the expectations your audience will have about your topic. Consider, for a moment, an after-dinner speech. What would you expect from that? Entertainment? Humour? Stories? Compare that to your expectations for a seminar on the latest changes in tax laws. Factual? Detailed? Dull?

I'm not saying that it's impossible (or indeed wrong) to make a tax seminar entertaining, it's more that your audience will have certain expectations about what you'll be talking about (and how) and that these considerations need to be taken into account when you are thinking about how to create your presentation.

The final aspect to consider here is how much your audience knows about your topic. You would create a very different presentation for an audience who know very little about your topic compared to the one that you would create for an audience who is knowledgeable in that area. If you pitch your presentation at the wrong level, it won't go as well as it could.

This also links back to your audience's expectations about the depth to which your presentation will go. "Beginner's", "overview", "introductory", "advanced", "expert" and "master": all of these words imply the depth to which your presentation will go and will set expectations with your audience about what it will contain and for whom it is therefore appropriate. It's very important that the reality matches the expectation...

And as a final observation, there is also a link back here to the audience's perspective on you. People might be more inclined to come and listen to you if they know you, if they know you're an interesting speaker or if you have a reputation for knowing what you are talking about. So it might not be the topic per se that draws them in, it might be you!

In summary:

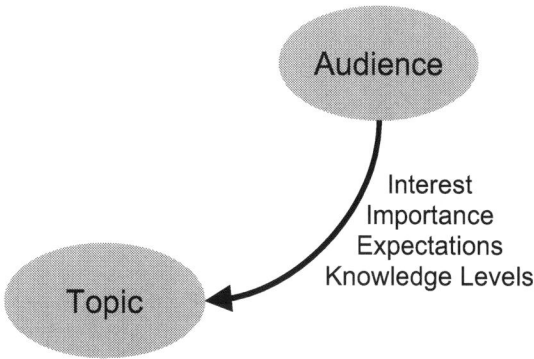

Your audience's perspective on itself

If you consider your audience as a collection of individuals and reflect on the answers to the questions you have asked about them in the previous sections, then you might get differences and you might get similarities. For example, your audience members might be from different companies or the same one. They might be from different industries or the same sector. There might be a range of knowledge levels or they might all be at roughly the same level.

So it's important to consider the variations and commonalities within the audience as a whole and to take that into account when you are creating your content.

There are, however, more aspects to think about here when investigating the nature of your audience. Things to consider here are, for example:

- How well do they know each other?
- What is their relationship to other audience members? For example:
    - Are they colleagues, collaborators or competitors?
    - Are there hierarchies/pecking orders?
    - Do they feel like one collective audience or a collection of smaller groups?
    - What are they expecting from each other?

Whilst you can't necessarily cater for each individual audience member, it is important to look at how the audience will interact with itself and what that means for you as the speaker and how you then design and deliver your content. Ironically, the larger your audience, the more generalised your considerations will become and so this isn't as daunting in practice as it may appear in theory.

In summary:

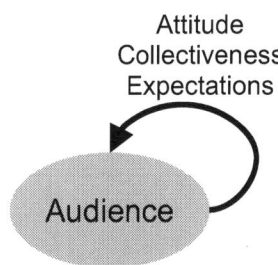

Attitude
Collectiveness
Expectations

Your perspective on the topic

Here's a definition of credential:

> a qualification, achievement, quality or aspect of a person's background, especially when used to indicate their suitability for something

I like this definition of a credential as it brings into scope more than just your qualifications and the list of letters after your name.

That being said, part of your credentials with regards to your topic are any qualifications that you have that are relevant to that area. There's nothing quite like a list of letters after your name to imply that you know what you're talking about!

These qualifications and letters will get noticed by your potential audience but what they mean to your audience may differ. For some, they will reinforce the expectation that you know what you are talking about. For others, they might imply that your knowledge is more theoretical than practical, which may not work in your favour.

And that's why I like the definition above as it brings into play other things for people to use to gauge your suitability to be talking about this topic.

Your current job, your current company, what you have done before and where you have done it will all add together to build your credentials and credibility as a speaker on a particular topic. The experience you have and the experiences that you have had will all affect your audience's expectations of you as a speaker.

That is, of course, assuming that they know this!

So when you are looking forward to your next presentation, have a think about what credentials you would like to portray to your audience in relation to the topic and then ensure that they have access to this information. How you do this will potentially differ from presentation to presentation but it is important that it is done so that your audience's expectations will be set correctly.

If you are a professional speaker then establishing your credentials is massively important, especially with the person who might be booking you for the presentation. Also, if you are being introduced by someone else, a best practice tip is to provide that person with the actual words that you would like them to use to introduce you. It's the best way of ensuring that things are going well before you even start your presentation...

The other aspect to consider here is your knowledge level of the topic. This one, however, is very straightforward: know what you are talking about!

In fact, know *more* than what you are talking about as that will give you a "buffer", some breathing space just in case you need it for any questions that go beyond the scope of what you are talking about.

Clearly you can't know everything but you need to know enough or more precisely, more than enough.

There is therefore effectively a minimal level of credentials, experience and knowledge that you need to have to be competent, comfortable and confident in speaking about your topic.

There is no doubt that if you do know what you are talking about, if you meet or surpass those levels, you will feel more confident both when you are looking ahead to the presentation and when you are actually delivering it.

But what if you don't meet those minimum levels? What can you do?

I appreciate that it sounds like an obvious question but, in reality, there are two answers.

The first is to do what you need to do to increase those levels. Study, research, observations, whatever the alternatives might be to attain the required levels. In effect, you're doing extra preparation for your presentation.

Referring back to earlier in the book, you're lengthening the **Preparation** (**P**) leg of your **CAPS** stool.

The second option is to do nothing (or not enough), to have a **P** leg on your stool that's too short. Wonky stool anyone?

The choice is yours and that links in with the final consideration in the YAT Triangle, your perspective on yourself, which I'll get to in a moment..

In summary:

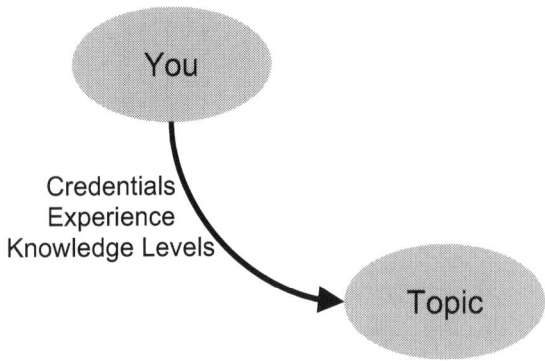

Your perspective on yourself

I call this the "Botheredness Loop".

There are a number of things to consider here:

- How bothered are you to think about your audience and their relationship with you and your topic?
- How bothered are you to be prepared, to be ready?
- How bothered are you to develop the skills and techniques required to be a better presenter?

The more bothered you are about the above, the better your presentation will be, the better impression you will make for yourself (and your company).
The reverse is also true if you are less bothered.

And it's no coincidence that the three bullet points above map to the **Audience** (**A**), **Preparation** (**P**) and **Skills** (**S**) considerations in the **CAPS** Framework. By implication therefore, the more bothered you are, the more confident you will be because you'll be a better presenter.

In summary:

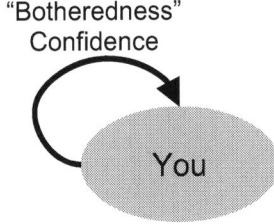

Recap

How you will go about approaching your presentation will therefore be affected by all of the perspectives of the YAT Triangle:

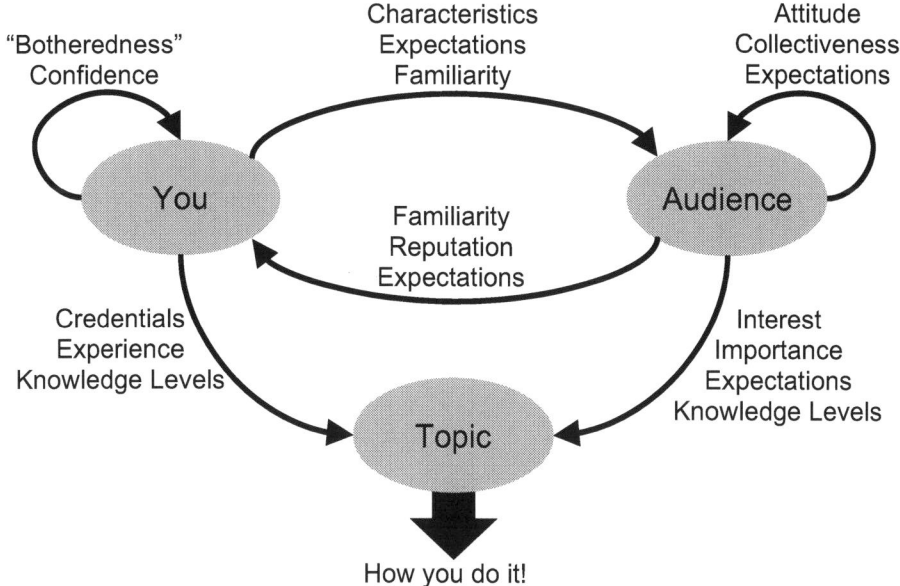

How you do it!

The more you consider these relationships, the more you think "audience first", the better your presentation will be, for your audience and ultimately therefore for you.

 *I have created a worksheet to help you to consider these relationships in more detail when you are creating your own presentations. You can download this worksheet from the Resources section of my website: www.intercog.co.uk.*

Online Considerations

Let's look at each aspect in turn.

Your perspective on your audience

These considerations remain mainly unchanged.

What will change potentially will be your expectations of that audience with respect to how much they might be willing to interact with you as you are now physically separated from them.

Also, if you are recording your presentation for later offline consumption, you will have no interaction with your audience which will affect how you create and deliver your presentation.

Your audience's perspective on you

This all applies to online presenting.

What also applies is your reputation for presenting online and any associated content. If you are known for being an interesting speaker regardless of the medium then that will help with your audience's reception of your presentations, not only in terms of how well they are received but also how many people will be watching.

Your audience's perspective on the topic

This is the same as the mode of delivery does not affect this.

Your audience's perspective on itself

This is perhaps where the biggest difference is.

It is highly unlikely that an audience that is physically disparate will have the same collective feeling as one that is in the room with you. It is also the case that the audience might not actually know who else is there due to the technology that is being used.

It's also possible that your audience might actually be only a single person, either because that's how it feels to them when they are watching you live (but remotely) or because they are watching your recording at a later date.

Your perspective on the topic

Everything here is still applicable to an online presentation.

Your perspective on yourself

You still need to be bothered and there is one more aspect about which you need to be bothered – technology!

I'm not suggesting that you have to be an expert in the technology that you will be using to deliver but you do need to be proficient and you do need to be practiced. The more you practise, the better you will get and the more confident you will feel using that technology (sound familiar?).

Simply put, the goal is for the technology to not get in the way of your message.

When Larry Met Ali

For distilling your core message into its simplest essence.

Picture the scene.

You have just finished your presentation at an important conference or a big meeting and, even by your own high standards, it has gone very well.

Larry, who listened intently and enjoyed what you said, is now suffering from having had too much coffee earlier and desperately needs a comfort break. He slips out of the room in search of some much-needed relief.

Ali, however, had to take an urgent business call and so missed your presentation. With the call now finished, she is on her way back towards the main room and she sees Larry coming the other way. Curious to know what she has missed, she stops Larry and asks him, "What did they say?"

Larry *really* needs to relieve himself of his excess coffee and has just about enough time (and control) for a single sentence.

So what would you like him to say?

Thinking about your message in this way allows you to focus on what the core of what you want to say is. What do you want people to remember and take away with them about what you said? What do you want them to do as a result of your presentation?

You will have an idea of what you want this core message to be when you start the process of putting your presentation together. You will potentially tweak it as you go through but it's crucially important to keep an eye on that core message or you run the risk of your presentation ending up being unfocussed, hard to follow and therefore eminently forgettable.

So as you are thinking about your presentation, think about what you would like to happen when Larry meets Ali. Keep it in mind and come back to it regularly.

It's only a simple framework but it's highly effective at keeping you focussed on what you want your core message to be.

Online Considerations

This analogy's point still holds: your presentation needs to have a clear message regardless of how you are delivering it.

The PRESENTER Framework

For creating interesting, understandable and memorable content for your presentations.

The **PRESENTER** Framework is a nine-part acronymic guide.

It represents a step-by-step, sequential approach to take when creating the content of a presentation, to help to make it interesting, understandable and memorable.

Let's examine each letter in turn.

PRESENTER

Start with why.

Therefore, the **P** stands for "What is the **Purpose** of your presentation?"

Or, putting it another way:

- Why are you giving the presentation?
- What are your goals/objectives?
- What are you aiming to achieve?

These are three questions that help you to achieve clarity on your objectives.

Here are five more questions that look at it more from your audience's perspective:

- What do you want people to take away with them?
- What would you like people to do as a result of your presentation?
- What would you like people to do differently after they leave?
- Why have you been asked to speak?
- Why would anyone in the audience want to listen to you?

Looking at it this way round is more akin to thinking about what your audience would like or need to hear as opposed to what you would like or need to say. Again, it's about thinking about your audience first.

I have created a worksheet to help you to address these questions when you are creating your own presentations. You can download this worksheet from the Resources section of my website: www.intercog.co.uk.

Knowing what you are aiming to achieve is massively important as is working that out right here up front at the start of the process. It's very difficult to hit a target when you don't know what it looks like or even where it is!

And while you are working out your purpose, remember when Larry met Ali as this is where you are starting to define that core message for your presentation.

p<u>R</u>ESENTER

The next step in the process is to consider your **Recipients**, i.e. those people who will be on the receiving end of your presentation, i.e. your audience.

There's not much to say here apart from to use the YAT Triangle (from earlier in the book).

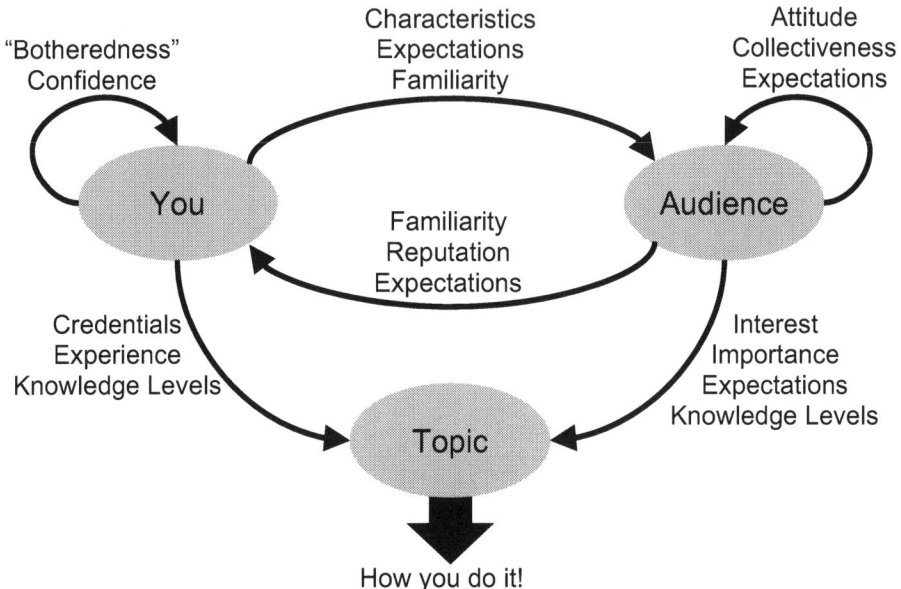

I have created a worksheet to help you to consider these relationships in more detail when you are creating your own presentations. You can download this worksheet from the Resources section of my website: www.intercog.co.uk.

pr<u>E</u>SENTER

What I am going to say next may seem counterintuitive. It might also seem like it is going against what I have said so far in this book.

Trust me, though, it works.

So, firstly, ignore any constraints or preconceptions you have about your presentation. It's time for some out of the box, blue-sky thinking.

Then, think of and capture **Everything** you could talk about relating to the topic of your presentation.

At this point ignore things like:

- how long you have to deliver your presentation
- the specifics of the knowledge levels of your audience
- any perceptions you have about what may or not be important

Include:

- things that you think are important
- things that you think might be useful
- stories
- examples
- anything and everything that is related to this topic that you could talk about if you had the time (and a willing audience)

Just blast it out in a brainstorm using whatever format you like: mind map, bullet points, whiteboard, post-it notes, whatever.

Leave it somewhere accessible and add to it over time as you think of more and more things that you could talk about. If possible, ask others to help with this potential content generation. They'll think of it from different angles and come up with things you haven't thought about. At this point, don't think about what you will actually talk about, how you are going to talk about it or in what order you'll do it. For now, just keep generating ideas on what you could include.

Keep things at a pretty high level at this point. The details will come later in the process.

Eventually, you will run out of ideas, or time. This latter consideration is important in that it's very easy to fall into the bottomless pit of idea generation and it consume a lot of time. Set yourself an "end time" for this part of the process that's reasonable, not only for allowing you time to generate the ideas, but also for allowing you time to complete the rest of the process before the presentation's delivery date!

PRE**S**ENTER

For a presentation to be easily understood by an audience, it has to have good **Structure**. Defining the structure for the presentation is therefore the next step.

There are many different structures that could be used for a presentation ranging from the simple "beginning, middle, end" approach to ones that are much more complex and refined.

> *The next section of this book is my **Content Pie Sandwich Framework**. It's my offering on how to structure a presentation for maximum effect for an audience and it works really well for that purpose. I'll save the details for then...*

Whichever structure you use (and I won't hold it against you if you don't use mine), that structure needs to facilitate making your presentation interesting, understandable and memorable for your audience.

Choose a structure that does this best for the circumstances of your presentation.

PRES**E**NTER

You are now in the position of having documented everything that you could possibly talk about and having decided on the structure of your presentation.

The next step is to get realistic and **Edit** your content to fit into your structure.

This is where constraints (e.g. time) and understanding of your audience (e.g. knowledge levels) come back into play. Keep an eye on these as you work out what gets included and what doesn't and in what order you will cover them. Also, focus on the purpose of your presentation and keep in mind your core message. Include only those things that will help you to achieve that.

A helpful tip in effectively doing this is to identify which are the most important things to include and to then put them into your presentation first. Then, if you still have space, add the next most important things and then the next until you have no more room. It's analogous to filling a jar with rocks. The best way of doing that is to put the big rocks in first...

You are flushing out your structure with content and by the end of this step you will know what you are going to say (probably still at a high level though) and the order in which you will talk about it.

PRESE**N**TER

The next step is to create the detail of what you are going to say. It's time to create your **Notes**.

I'm not talking here about the notes that you might use to help you to actually deliver the presentation. Creating those comes later in the process. I'm talking about the detail that you will talk about for each of the sections of your presentation.

Take some time to work out those details. Some presenters effectively create their script verbatim, others might use a more bulleted format and others prefer a more visual representation like a mind map. Use whichever format you prefer.

The goal here is to create the details of what you will actually say in your presentation, so the facts you will use, the stories you will tell, the examples you will give.

By the end of this step you will know exactly what you want to say. In fact, you could talk through your presentation if needed as you are very prepared by this stage in the process.

Clearly, though, at this point in the process you would not come across as well as in the actual presentation because when you do it for real you might use delivery aids (e.g. slides) to help you. I'll get to those in a moment...

The point here is that you know what you are going to say, how you are going to achieve the purpose of your presentation.

Doing it like this is also a safety net, it's protection against that potential nightmare situation – technology failure!

It might be a missing lead, broken projector or a dead laptop. Maybe even something more serious like a power cut. But whatever it is, it means that you can't use your technology. No slides, no videos, nothing!

It's OK though. You know what you want to say, so you can still say it. It won't be as slick as with those delivery aids that you've created (which I promise I will get to soon) but you will still be able to get your message across to your audience.

Doing it this way also means that you are not reliant on your delivery aids. They are not a crutch on which you lean and without which you'll fall down. You can survive without them. They are simply tools to help you to get your message across to your audience in a way that's even more interesting, even more understandable and even more memorable.

Think of this approach as being a bit like insurance. You are covered just in case things go wrong. And the nice thing about being insured is that it gives you the reassurance that you can cope and that, in turn, will give you more confidence.

*I'm not suggesting, though, that you take a carefree attitude regarding the availability and reliability of your technology. You need to think about this carefully and I have some thoughts on that later in the **Be Environmentally Aware** Framework.*

PRESEN**T**ER

The time has come to talk about the P word – PowerPoint!

But not about creating your slides – we're not quite there yet…
So why am I mentioning PowerPoint if I'm not going to be talking about creating slides? It's because, for this step in the framework, I'm borrowing a PowerPoint term around which the discussion is based. The term I am borrowing is **Template**.

And why am I borrowing this term? For two reasons.

The first reason is because of what a template is in PowerPoint and the ethos behind using one.

The second is because I needed a word beginning with **T** for the framework!

For those of you who know what a PowerPoint template is, please bear with me a moment.

For those of you that don't, a template is a construct in PowerPoint that allows for the definition of a consistent look and feel for a presentation. It allows for the defining of colours, graphics and fonts that will be used for the various different types of slides you might have in a presentation (e.g. title, content etc.). You define this once and then use it consistently across all of your slides. The goal of using a template is to make your presentation look professional and "all joined up".

Templates therefore separate the look and feel from the content itself and that's great because there are two steps in this framework too – one for the template creation and one for the content creation.

So if you're using slides, create a clear, consistent and clutter-free template, one that reflects you and your company.

There is, however, more to your look and feel than just your slide template.

What else might you be giving out to your audience? Notes, handouts, product samples, freebies?

What else might you be using as part of your presentation that your audience might see or use? Props, posters?

All of these need to be consistent with each other (and with your slides if you have them) so everything looks "joined up".

I appreciate that I'm stretching the template concept somewhat here but the principle still holds…

PRESENT**E**R

This next step is all about **Extracting** information.

You're now in the position that you know the "why", the "who" and the "what" for your presentation. It's time to consider the "how".

It's time to ask this question: "What do you need to create to help you to deliver your presentation?"

Your goal is to deliver an interesting, understandable and memorable presentation. What can you do, what can you use to make it even more interesting, even more understandable and even more memorable?

In other words, what "delivery aids" will you need?

Will you, for example:

- be using a slide presentation?
- be handing anything out?
- be using props?
- have any audience participation?
- be using delivery notes?

Some of these will need to contain information. Fortunately, you have the information already that you need to put in them, you have that in your notes (from the earlier step in the framework). All you need to do is extract the *relevant* information to create these delivery aids.

However, some of these delivery aids that you will create will be for your audience and some will be for you.

Delivery aids for your audience

Let's start with the most common delivery aid – slides (yes, the time to talk about slides has finally arrived!).

What *needs* to go on the slide to help your audience to understand what you are saying at that point in your presentation? And, by implication, what doesn't need to be there (and shouldn't be)?

Remember: your slides are for your audience, not for you. They are there to help your audience to understand your message.

Clearly though, well designed slides will also potentially help to serve as prompts/cues for you to help you when delivering your presentation but that's just a side-effect of good slides, not the main reason for creating them.

This is why it is only now that you should be creating slides. If slides are created any earlier in the process it's far too easy to put information on those slides that is not helpful for your audience. I'm sure we've all witnessed presentations where the slides are far too wordy, where the presenter is in effect just reading what's on the slides. In most cases it's because the presenter has started with the slides and used them to collect their notes, i.e. what they are going to say.

(This is why I jokingly threaten to hit people over the head if they think of doing it!)

What you put on them is ultimately up to you but whatever you put on the slides make sure that it's:
- relevant to the point you are making
- helpful to your audience in understanding that point
- not distracting your audience from what you are saying

An audience should never be put in the position of having to choose between listening to you or reading what's on your slide!
How many slides you need will vary between presentations but only create those you need. It might be the case that you decide that for a particular presentation you don't need any slides to help you to get your message across and that's absolutely fine. Slides are not mandatory.

If you do create slides then most of them will be "content" slides and some will be "structural" slides, e.g. your title slide, agenda slide, "Thank You" slide etc.

> *I have created a video discussing the different types of "structural" slides that you might need to create for a presentation. That video can be downloaded from the Resources section of my website: www.intercog.co.uk.*

And whilst we're talking about slides, here's a question for you: Which of your slides will probably be displayed for the longest?

It's your title slide.

It will be up there right at the start potentially even before people enter the room. If you're nice and early and set up accordingly, your title slide might be on display for over 10 minutes. That's a long time for your audience to notice it.

It's your first chance to entice your audience and increase their interest level in your presentation. Use that "free advertising" time wisely.

So what exactly will the title of your presentation be, how does it link to your purpose and how does it support your core message, your "When Larry met Ali" moment?

Think carefully therefore about what you are going to put on that slide.

> *One of the workshops that I deliver is around confidence and how to increase it. It's a collection of tips, tricks and techniques for being more confident. The title of my workshop could therefore quite reasonably have been: "Tips, tricks and techniques for being more confident."*
>
> *But that's not what my title was. Instead, I used: "You will leave this workshop more confident than when you arrived." It's a much more enticing title, it intrigues the audience into how I'm going to achieve that and directly supports the main purpose of the workshop: to help people to be more confident.*

There are other things that you could use to help your audience to be interested in, understand and remember your presentation. You could use, for example:

- handouts
- posters
- props
- audience participation

> *It's a personal favourite of mine to use the audience themselves as props where appropriate. It helps to keep them interested, if for no other reason than it keeps them on their toes in case they are next! It also can be a lot of fun, for them and for me...*

Again you can use whatever you would like to here as long as it's helpful for the audience.

When choosing your delivery aids, also bear in mind:
- their appropriateness for your audience
- their appropriateness for the topic
- your own ability and confidence to use them
    - the more you use them, the better you will become at using them and the more confident you will be when using them
- their purpose, for example:
    - the purpose of your slides is very different from the purpose of a reference document that is handed out
    - don't therefore use your slides as a reference handout or, even worse, your reference handout as slides

Delivery aids for you

So far in this step, all of the conversation has been about what you can create to help your audience to take in your presentation. There are, however, also things that you can create to help you to deliver it well.

Many speakers use notes to help them to deliver their presentations. Those notes come in many shapes and forms and are ultimately a personal preference. Again though, what needs to be put on any such notes is information that is extracted from the full notes you created earlier in the process.

Only include what you need to help you to deliver your presentation well. That may therefore be, for example:

- some text (not a lot!)
- key words
- diagrams
- pictures
- key facts and figures

I don't advocate having your full notes verbatim as the delivery aid, though, as this comes across as far too scripted. It's also a lot easier to lose your place (and therefore find it again!). They also tend to negatively affect eye contact with the audience, which I'll come back to in a moment.

Again, what you put these notes on is up to you but I would suggest that thicker is better! Card flops around less than paper and it also rustles less. iPads, etc., don't rustle at all!

Also, smaller is better too as it covers less of you up and also exaggerates any nervous shakes less. There's nothing like a few sheets of A4 paper shaking in your hands to make you look nervous!

Some people would argue that good presenters shouldn't be using notes at all. They should have the presentation so well prepared that they don't need any notes to refer to whilst they are delivering it.

And for professional speakers that's probably true!

But for the rest of us mortals, using notes is perfectly acceptable as long as they are used well.

And what does "using them well" mean? That's simply that using the notes does not distract the audience from the message. My observations of watching many people present is that you only actually notice people using notes if they use them badly. So if they, for example:

- read from them verbatim
- hold them up in front of them so the audience can't see their face

- look down at them rather than look up at the audience
- rustle them
- or drop them

In these circumstances, you will notice the notes as they are distracting for the audience.

But used well, they are almost invisible to your audience and a great aid to your delivery!

Technology can also potentially help with your speaker aids if you are using slides. Most presentation software has the ability to display speaker notes that only you can see as well as possibly the next slide/animation in your presentation. A *well-placed* laptop or monitor can then allow you to use these rather than physical aids.

*Notice the emphasis on well-placed. I'll come back to this in more detail in the **SPEAKER** Framework.*

PRESENTE**R**

The final step is to **Rehearse** your presentation, to practise it.

They say that "practice makes perfect" but I don't think it does (as there is always room for improvement).

However, practice does make better and the more practice, the better!

Make that practice as realistic as possible, as close as you can to the situation you will be in when you actually deliver your presentation. Therefore:

- practise with your delivery aids, whatever they may be
- visualise your audience in front of you
- use the tips, tricks and techniques of the **SPEAKER** Framework to help you to do that with confidence

Rehearsing your presentation will allow you to refine it, to ensure that it is achieving your purpose for delivering it and, importantly, to ensure that you can do it in the time that you have to do it.

But which part of your presentation is the most important, the part that you need to therefore practise the most?

Whilst you might say "all of it", in reality there are two answers to this question: the beginning and the end. As they are the most important parts of your presentation, they are therefore the parts that you need to practise the most.

> *Practising your beginning and your ending more than the middle also supports the recognised reality regarding what your audience will remember most: the beginning, the end and only then a few of the interesting bits in the middle!*

Thinking about your beginning first then, there are a number of reasons why you need to practise and practise and practise this.

The first reason is that you only get one chance to make a first impression so you need to make sure it's a good one!

The second reason is to do with familiarity. It's highly likely that the main content in your presentation is the part that is most familiar to you as you probably talk about it on a daily basis. It is therefore probably the easiest for you to talk about in your presentation.

Whatever it is that you say before getting to that comfortable content is, however, not naturally familiar to you. It's something that you have created for this presentation to get it off to a great start. To make it more familiar, to become more comfortable and effective in delivering it, you therefore need to practise it more.

And the other reasons are all about confidence. If you have practised your introduction, if you are ready and prepared, you can take confidence from that. It's the **Preparation (P)** in the **CAPS** Framework.

Also, before your actual delivery, if you take a moment to consciously remember that you have practised, that you are ready and that you are prepared, you'll take even more confidence from that too.

If you take this extra confidence into your delivery, your beginning will go even better. And when your beginning goes well, you will take the increased confidence from that into the rest of your presentation and that will go better too. This snowballing confidence effect all stems from practising your beginning and practising it lots.

The reason for also practising your ending a lot is very simple: you want to end with a focused bang, with your core message ringing loud and clear in the ears of your audience. In other words, make it very clear and obvious what Larry would say to Ali! Also, as with your beginning, your closing will be less familiar to you and so will require more practice to hone it.

> *Fortunately, the ability to record presentations (or the practising of them) is relatively straightforward with modern technology these days. Watching yourself back on recordings, although it might feel a bit odd, is a great way of reflecting on your delivery and improving over time. You could also ask others for feedback too!*

Recap

Putting it all together, here's a summary of the **PRESENTER** Framework:

Determine the **P**urpose of your presentation
Identify and analyse the **R**ecipients of your presentation
Work out **E**verything you could talk about
Decide on the **S**tructure of your presentation
Edit the content to fit the structure
Create your **N**otes
Decide on your **T**emplate (look and feel)
Make delivery aids by **E**xtracting information
Rehearse (rehearse, rehearse)

Online Considerations

Let's look at each step in turn.

Determine the Purpose of your presentation

This still holds true for online presenting.

Identify and analyse the Recipients of your presentation

Taking an audience-first approach is also still a good idea albeit there are some extra considerations for online delivery as discussed previously in the **YAT Triangle** Framework.

Work out Everything you could talk about

This is still a valid approach.

Decide on the Structure of your presentation

Your presentation will need to have a good structure to help it to be interesting, understandable and memorable.

As there is less of a direct connection with an online or remote audience, there is a strong argument that your presentation will need to have an even clearer structure to help your audience "stay with you" during your presentation.

Edit the content to fit the structure

Your content still needs to fit!

Create your Notes

You still need to know what you are going to say and so this step is still important.

Decide on your Template (look and feel)

This still applies as you would want to have a consistent approach to what you will "give" to your audience, although the actual way that you "give" things to your audience might change, e.g. from a physical handout to an emailed attachment or downloadable resource.

Make delivery aids by Extracting information

This is where there is the most difference between in-person and online delivery.

If you are using a slide presentation then the core considerations for what goes onto those slides remain as above. You might, however, need some more structural slides to help guide your audience through the presentation.

But what about the other delivery aids that you create for your audience? How will they apply if you are not delivering in person? For each of those aids you need to evaluate if it can still be used.

For some, you might still be able to use them, e.g. a physical prop may still be able to be used. Slight changes might need to be made to allow you to do this for other aids though. For example, a physical handout that you would have used in person might need to be created as an electronic document that can be made available to the audience via a suitable route, e.g. as an email attachment or downloadable resource.

For others, you might need to find alternatives. For example, a physical prop may no longer be viable due to its size, perhaps, and so an electronic version may be needed instead, whether that be something that is made available to your audience or perhaps incorporated into your slides for example. If you were planning on using a flipchart and that is no longer practical, then how are you going to address that? Do you change your presentation to not include that section, do that section in another way or use a technological solution to provide a "virtual" flipchart?

> *Going back to my personal favourite of using the audience themselves as props where appropriate, this may still be possible if the technology allows for it, you are knowledgeable enough in how to use that technology and have the confidence to do it!*

With regard to the delivery aids that you create for yourself, the principle still holds that you are creating things that will help you to deliver the presentation well. You still need therefore to carefully consider what you create and how you use it.

There is, however, one big difference between presenting in person and online. When you are there in person your audience can see you and everything around you whereas when you are presenting online, your audience can only see what you let them see through your camera. This means that you can consciously and deliberately "hide" things out of view of your audience that you can then use to help you to deliver your presentation, things that you couldn't use if you were presenting in person.

This gives you the opportunity to, for example:

- use multiple screens
- have things/applications open on your screen(s)
- stick things to your screen(s)
- have larger reference sheets around your screen with extra information on them, e.g. the structure/flow of the presentation, key points, important facts and figures etc.

*It's important that anything you have around your screen does not distract your attention from your audience, however, as you still need to be looking at them through the camera. There are more considerations about this in the **SPEAKER** Framework.*

The other main difference about what you need to consider when presenting online is to do with the environment in which you present, or more precisely, what you need to have and whose responsibility it is for providing it. These are not really delivery aids as such but it's probable that you will be thinking about them as you consider the delivery aids that you need to create.

*I'll talk about the delivery environment for presenting both in person and online in the **Be Environmentally Aware** Framework later.*

Rehearse (rehearse, rehearse)

Everything that I said above regarding practising your presentation still applies. What also applies when delivering online is that you need to practise using the technology so that it does not interfere with your delivery.

Part of that practice is to ensure that the technology itself is used effectively.

Part of that practice, however, is more to do with becoming more comfortable in the art of delivering online. Many presenters find it hard to talk to a camera at first due to a perceived lack of connection with their audience. It takes time to develop the mindset to do this well and to therefore become comfortable doing it. And that's where practice comes in…

The Content Pie Sandwich

For structuring a presentation to ensure it is interesting, understandable and memorable.

Actually, the full name of this framework is the "Double-crusted Content Pie Sandwich with a Little Bit of Butter on Top and Bottom".

But that's just too much of a mouthful (pun intended) which is why I'll simply refer to it as the **Content Pie Sandwich**.

This **Content Pie Sandwich** is a guide that I first developed well over a decade ago and have massaged and tweaked a number of times since. Its goal is simply to help you to structure your content so that it's interesting, understandable and memorable for your audience and it's a proven approach to achieve this.

As with a real sandwich, there are a number of ingredients that go into it and those different ingredients come together to make the whole **Content Pie Sandwich** Framework. It looks like this:

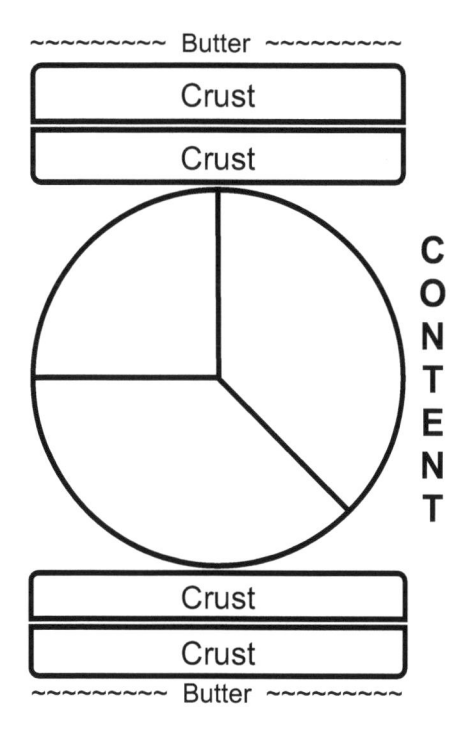

~~~~~~~~~ Butter ~~~~~~~~~

| Crust |
| Crust |

(pie chart with three segments) — CONTENT

| Crust |
| Crust |

~~~~~~~~~ Butter ~~~~~~~~~

The content pie is in the middle, with double crusts to make it a sandwich and a bit of butter on the top and the bottom. Let's look at each of the pieces in turn and put them together to make the finished article – just like you would if you were making a real sandwich…

The Content Pie

So let's start in the middle where the meat (or non-meat alternative) of the sandwich is. This is your content. Your content is divided up into different sections so it starts to look a bit like a pie, a Content Pie:

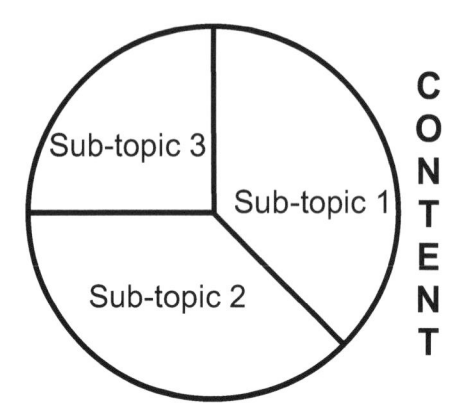

In her book "How to be brilliant at Public Speaking", Sarah Lloyd-Hughes also talks about a content pie. It was reading about Sarah's pie that sparked a few ideas in my head that complemented and extended my own version of a content pie. So our pies are different and similar all at the same time, in the same way apple pies and meat pies are!

Each of the pieces of the pie will be a sub-topic of the overall topic about which you are speaking.

You'll notice that the pie has three pieces. That's because the human brain likes things that come in threes. The world of advertising, entertainment and literature use this principle all of the time, for example:

- The Good, the Bad and the Ugly
- Location. Location. Location.
- To explore strange new worlds. To seek out new life and new civilizations. To boldly go where no one has gone before!
- The Fellowship of the Ring, The Two Towers, The Return of the King
    o (The Lord of the Rings)
- How to be Better at Presenting, How to be Better at Networking, How to be Better at Communicating
    o (The "***Interact*** better. ***Achieve*** more." Series)

I suspect you'll notice a lot more triplets like these now...

Splitting your content into three will therefore also work especially well for your presentation. In essence, what you are doing is taking your main topic and dividing it into three sub-topics:

Thinking back to the **PRESENTER** Framework, this is where you are **Editing** your content by looking at **Everything** you could talk about and working out what will fit and where. You'll naturally therefore start by deciding on your three sub-topics and start to include relevant content. (Put the big rocks in the jar first)

Depending on the time that you have for your presentation and the level of detail that you want to go into, you could subdivide a sub-topic into sub-sub-topics if needed:

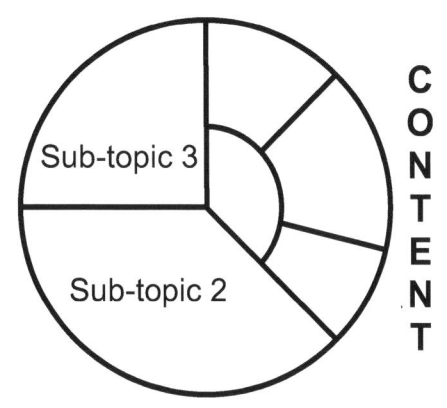

Notice again the division into three parts.

(For clarity purposes, I won't draw the sub-sub-topics on the later diagrams.)

By doing this you will end up with a mapping of your content into the structure which will define what you're going to talk about and in what order. Also, as the amount of content will vary by section, each of the pieces of the pie will be different sizes which will give you an idea of how long it will take to talk about each section.

So that's the Content Pie, let's now make it a sandwich.

The Inner Crusts

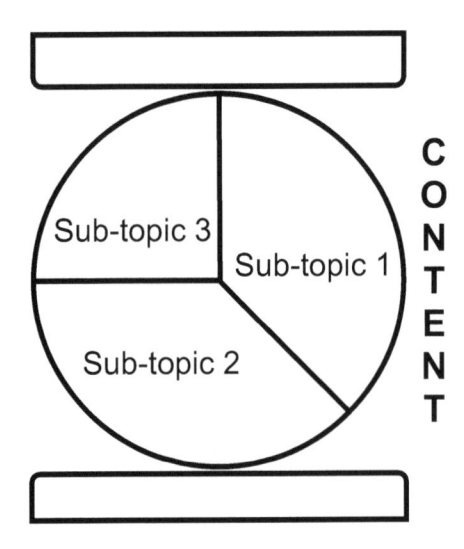

```
         ┌─────────────┐
         │             │
        ╱───────────────╲
       ╱                 ╲   C
      │  Sub-topic 3      │  O
      │          Sub-topic 1│ N
      │─────────          │  T
      │                   │  E
      │    Sub-topic 2    │  N
       ╲                 ╱   T
        ╲───────────────╱
         │             │
         └─────────────┘
```

As with any sandwich, we have a crust (i.e. bread) on the top and on the bottom. In the context of this sandwich, each crust has a particular function.

The crust on the top is your introduction where you tell your audience what you are going to tell them. It's a very simple and short section as its purpose is really just to set the scene with your audience to let them know what's coming up.

Audiences like to know this.

Firstly, it sets their expectations for what's coming up and their anticipations for the parts of the presentation that are of most interest and importance to them.

Secondly, it helps them to understand what you'll be saying because they now have a plan in their heads of how it's going to happen. They have a route map of the journey on which you're going to take them during your presentation which you can then use to guide them through it. (more on that in a moment)

So, an introduction might therefore be simply something along the lines of:

> *Today I'm going to start by giving you a quick overview of our company. (Sub-topic 1)*
>
> *Then I'll go into more detail about what we see your training requirements as being. (Sub-topic 2)*
>
> *And I'll finish off by taking you through how we can meet those training needs for you. (Sub-topic 3)*

Tell them what you're going to tell them!

The bottom crust is your summary where you tell them what you have just told them. It's just a brief recap to remind them of the journey they have been on.

Again it's simple and short:

So there we are!

I've told you a bit about us as a company (Sub-topic 1), what we see your training requirements as being (Sub-topic 2) and how we can meet those needs for you. (Sub-topic 3)

Basically, tell them what you've just told them!

So looking at the sandwich as it stands at the moment it's like this:

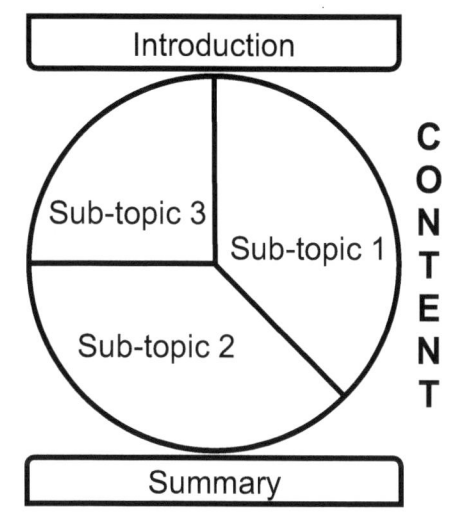

```
          Introduction
      ┌─────────────────┐
      │                 │  C
      │                 │  O
      │  Sub-topic 3    │  N
      │      Sub-topic 1│  T
      │                 │  E
      │  Sub-topic 2    │  N
      │                 │  T
      └─────────────────┘
            Summary
```

Or, to put it another way:

- tell them what you're going to tell them
- tell them
- tell them what you've just told them

No surprises therefore that the main part of your presentation is also split into three.

As a final comment on this I'd like to come back to the journey on which you will be taking your audience and how you can guide them along it to help them to keep track of where they are and where they are going next.

This is where the radial lines of the pie come into it. Those lines present you with opportunities to briefly refer to the route map, to update your audience with where they are on the journey so they can keep track. They can also act as links between the sections and reminders of what's coming next.

So, carrying on with the example above, those links (i.e. the radial lines) could be as simple as this (I'm repeating the introduction and summary for context):

(Introduction)

Today I'm going to start by giving you a quick overview of our company.

Then I'll go into more detail about what we see your training requirements as being.

And I'll finish off by taking you through how we can meet those training needs for you.

So who are we? (The vertical radial line that leads into Sub-topic 1)

(Deliver Sub-topic 1)
So that's a bit about us. I'd like to now talk about what we see your training requirements as being. (The radial line between Sub-topic 1 and Sub-topic 2)

(Deliver Sub-topic 2)

Those are your requirements as we see them. This is how we can meet those needs for you. (The radial line between Sub-topic 2 and Sub-topic 3)

(Deliver Sub-topic 3)

(Summary)

So there we are!

I've told you a bit about us as a company, what we see your training requirements as being and how we can meet those needs for you.

> **T** *If your presentation is of a sufficient length or depth, you could also have mini-agenda slides at those points where you transition between sub-topics to very clearly show where you are in the presentation, where the audience is along the journey. Those slides would double as handy reminders for you too!*

> **V** *I have created a video discussing the different types of "structural" slides that you might need to create for a presentation. That video can be downloaded from the Resources section of my website: www.intercog.co.uk*

Audiences that get lost in a presentation will struggle to understand it. To prevent that from happening, the presentation needs to be well structured and your audience needs to be well guided through that structure. That's what this part of the framework is really all about.

Now you might be thinking that this looks OK for the structure of a presentation. What else is needed?

Clearly I believe that something else is needed or else there wouldn't be two more crusts and some butter!

The Top Outer Crust and Top Butter

So let's add the top outer crust and its butter:

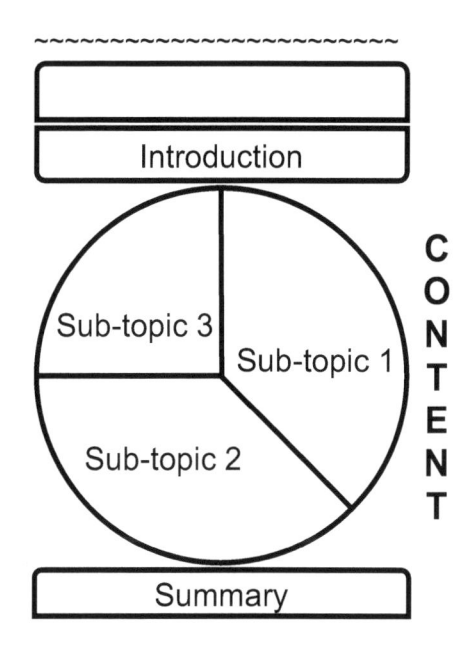

```
~~~~~~~~~~~~~~~~~~~~~~~~~
┌─────────────────────────┐
│                         │
└─────────────────────────┘
┌─────────────────────────┐
│      Introduction       │
└─────────────────────────┘
         _____          C
        /     |     \         O
       / Sub- |      \        N
      | topic3| Sub-  |       T
      |-------|topic 1|       E
       \      |      /        N
        \ Sub-topic 2/        T
         _____/
┌─────────────────────────┐
│        Summary          │
└─────────────────────────┘
```

So what might be in that top outer crust?

What might you need to do before telling your audience what you're going to talk about?

Possible answers that you might have thought of could be:

- introduce yourself
- say which company you're from
- thank the organisers for inviting you to speak
- etc.

They are all great answers but that's actually what the top bit of butter is for. The top bit of butter is how you slide into the presentation by saying something that's easy for you to say.

You might say something like:

Hi!

I'm Mike Grocott from Intercog and I'd like to thank Staffordshire Chambers for asking me to speak here today.

In fact, if you've been introduced by somebody else, all you really need to say is "Thank you".

So if that's the top bit of butter, what's the top outer crust for? If you've done your top bit of butter and you're off and running in your presentation, what do you do next *before* your introduction?

Clearly I'm intending for something to be there as there's a crust there in place for it…

That top outer crust is for your Attention Grabber.

So what do I mean by an Attention Grabber and why do you need one?

An Attention Grabber is something that you do and/or say that makes your audience want to listen to you. It piques their curiosity and makes them interested in your presentation. It breaks the ice and warms the audience up for you.

And you do it because a presentation is much better received if people actually want to listen to you, if they think that it will be interesting. Of course, some of your audience will arrive interested already but this is your opportunity to capture everyone's attention and get them ready to listen.

So what to do?

There are many options here, including:

- telling a story
- relating a metaphor
- saying something humorous
- asking the audience questions
- getting the audience to do something
- shocking the audience in some way

The key thing is to choose something that's *appropriate* for your audience and for the occasion of your presentation.

It's also possible that your Attention Grabber links to your core message but it doesn't have to necessarily.

So don't just plough into your introduction. Do something that will make them want to listen to you!

T *It might take you a while to come up with your Attention Grabber as sometimes they come easily and sometimes they don't! If you are struggling to come up with one, though, don't worry. It will come to you...*

So as to not break the flow of this part of the book, I've listed later in this chapter a number of examples of Attention Grabbers that I've seen and helped people to come up with in the past.

The Bottom Outer Crust

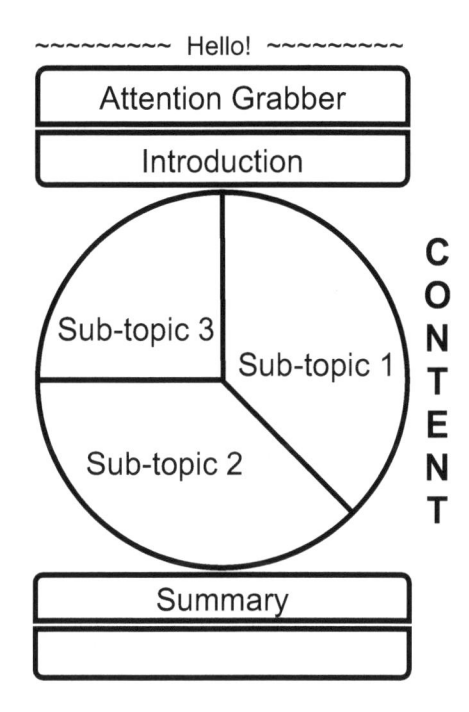

~~~~~~~~~ Hello! ~~~~~~~~~

```
┌─────────────────────────┐
│   Attention Grabber     │
├─────────────────────────┤
│     Introduction        │
└─────────────────────────┘
```

Sub-topic 3 | Sub-topic 1
Sub-topic 2

C O N T E N T

```
┌─────────────────────────┐
│       Summary           │
├─────────────────────────┤
│                         │
└─────────────────────────┘
```

And in the same way, don't get to the end of your summary and then just stop. Don't forget, as well as what you say first, what you say last is the most remembered part of your presentation, so take that opportunity to leave your audience with something memorable.

That's what the bottom crust is for.

I refer to this crust as your Attention Focuser. It might be linked to your Attention Grabber, although it doesn't have to be. Linking them together can often work well as it provides some symmetry to your presentation, topping and tailing it with related content. That being said, don't sacrifice a great Attention Grabber just so that you can link these two crusts together.

However. the one thing that your Attention Focuser must link to is your core message. Remember Larry? Your core message needs to be clear and ringing in his ears as he hurries off to his destination.

This crust also provides you with a great opportunity for a call to action, if that's the purpose of your presentation. What would you like your audience to do now or in the future as a result of your presentation? What is your challenge to them?

This is the time and the place to make that clear, the time when it has the most impact.

And because you want this message to be ringing in people's ears, don't end with a Q&A session. Don't end with a section that's out of your control, that might dilute your message or distract people from it.

If you want people to have the opportunity to ask questions, build that time into your Content Pie or do it *between* the bottom crusts, i.e. after the Summary but before your Attention Focuser. That way you will still be able to finish with your core message, with you in control of what your audience will be hearing.

So that just leaves us with the bit of butter on the bottom.

The Butter on the Bottom

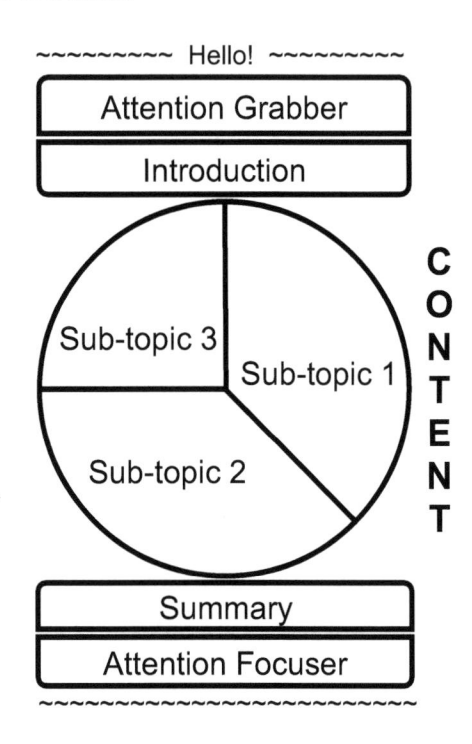

~~~~~~~~~ Hello! ~~~~~~~~~

Attention Grabber

Introduction

Sub-topic 3
Sub-topic 1
Sub-topic 2

CONTENT

Summary

Attention Focuser

~~~~~~~~~~~~~~~~~~~~~~~~

In the same way the butter at the top was to slide you easily into your presentation, this butter allows you to finally tie things up straightforwardly and slide out of your presentation. All you need to do here is to smile, quickly thank again anyone you need to and then stop talking!

Recap

So there you have it!

The **Content Pie Sandwich** or, to give it its full name once more: The Double-crusted Content Pie Sandwich with a Little Bit of Butter on Top and Bottom.

Here it is in its full glory:

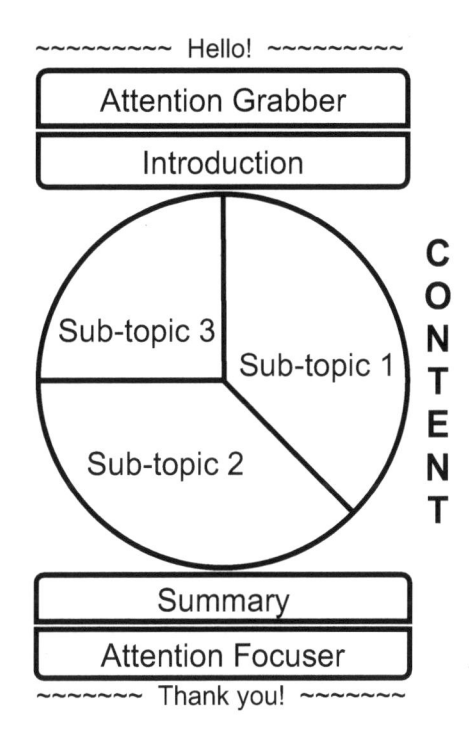

```
~~~~~~~~ Hello! ~~~~~~~~
┌─────────────────────────┐
│    Attention Grabber    │
├─────────────────────────┤
│      Introduction       │
└─────────────────────────┘
         ╱───────╲            C
       ╱           ╲          O
     │ Sub-topic 3  │         N
     │      ╲───────│         T
     │ Sub-topic 1  │         E
     │ Sub-topic 2  │         N
       ╲           ╱          T
         ╲───────╱
┌─────────────────────────┐
│         Summary         │
├─────────────────────────┤
│    Attention Focuser    │
└─────────────────────────┘
~~~~~~~ Thank you! ~~~~~~~
```

Yes, it's a bit of a mouthful. (All good sandwiches are!)

And yes, there are a number of parts to it.

But yes, it works!

*I have created a blank template for you to use when you are creating your own presentations using the **Content Pie Sandwich** Framework for structure. You can download that template from the Resources section of my website: www.intercog.co.uk.*

Online Considerations

The **Content Pie Sandwich** Framework is as equally applicable to online delivery as it is to in-person delivery.

The only real difference is that the Attention Grabber needs to be even more grabbing online, especially if it is a recording on a platform such as YouTube. How you start needs to really grab the attention of the audience and make them really want to stay and watch. If it doesn't they will leave the online presentation or just simply select the next video being offered to them.

After all, it's a lot easier to drop out of an online session or select the next video than it is to physically get up and leave the audience during an in-person presentation…

Examples: Attention Grabbers

I have witnessed many really good Attention Grabbers over the years and seen a few shockers too!

The examples below are some of my favourites (good ones of course!).

NOTE: What you see below are my best recollections of what was said. Although these words might not be the actual originals, therefore, the principle of their being good Attention Grabbers remains.

The Rt Hon Sir John Major KG CH

Sir John Major was the Prime Minister of the UK from 1990 to 1997. During that time he had a demeanour of considered seriousness, although to be fair, it was a serious job he had to do!

I saw Sir John Major speak at Computer Associates' CA-World conference in July 1997, only a few months after he had lost the election and therefore the position of Prime Minister. There were several thousand of us in the audience ready to hear him speak. Every one of us in the audience had expectations of what he would be like as he was a public figure and had been on the news a lot in the previous few years. Although I didn't actually ask anyone there, it would have been fairly safe to assume that we were expecting more "considered seriousness", so not perhaps the most exciting or engaging of speeches. This was because we "knew" him, or at least we thought we did.

How wrong we were!

This is how Sir John Major opened his speech:

> *I would like to thank Computer Associates for inviting me here to speak to you today. I would also like to thank the British public for making it possible.*

That somewhat self-deprecating joke was completely unexpected and actually very funny - many people laughed!

And everyone thought, "Hold on, this might not be like what we were expecting. Let's see what he has to say…"

Because of this attention-grabbing, very surprising opener, Sir John Major's audience now really wanted to listen. He had piqued their curiosity and they were very much looking forward to hearing what he had to say.

In fact, it was a very entertaining speech and one of the best I ever heard over the many years that I attended those conferences.

Steve Cunningham

Steve Cunningham is an inspirational motivational speaker.

He went blind at the age of 12 but has done many amazing things since then. At the time of hearing Steve speak:

- he held the world land speed record (for driving a car) for a blind person
- he held the onshore and offshore powerboat world records for a blind person
- he had flown a plane around the UK coastline

At the event, we were all sitting around our tables, waiting for Steve to speak. Here's his Attention Grabber:

> *Ladies and Gentlemen, please close your eyes.*
>
> *Now imagine that you are sitting in a top sportscar, with your eyes still closed.*
>
> *You're doing 172 MPH down a runway.*
>
> *You can hear the roar of the engine, the rush of the wind as you hurtle along and the vibration of the car all around you.*
>
> *Imagine that scene.*
>
> *Imagine what you'd be feeling.*
>
> *Now imagine that you were driving!*
>
> *Welcome to my world…*

To say that we were hooked would be an understatement!

Tony Scholes

Tony Scholes is the CEO of Stoke City Football Club.

In 2012, Tony Scholes was the guest speaker at the Spring Lunch of Finest, Staffordshire's premier networking organisation for the Professional Services sector.

Tony Scholes opened his speech like this.

> Thank you for asking me here to speak to you today.
>
> I have to admit, Ladies and Gentlemen, that I really struggled to work out what I should talk about today. I had a real mental block.
> So much so, I was sitting in my study with my head in my hands and an empty piece of paper on my desk when my son walked past the door. He could see that something was wrong and so asked, "What's up Dad?".
>
> "Oh, it's this speech I've got to do on Friday." I replied. "I don't know what to say.".
>
> "What's the speech?" my son enquired.
>
> "Finest have asked me to be their guest speaker at their Spring Lunch event."
>
> "Who are Finest?" my son continued.
>
> "Finest is the main networking organisation in Staffordshire for professional services organisations" I replied.
>
> "OK. So who's in Finest?"
>
> "Well it's people in professional services such as solicitors, accountants, architects, consultants, trainers and so on. People who sell their time and expertise to their clients."
>
> "And are they any good at it?" my son asked.
>
> "Oh yes, they are really successful companies."
>
> "OK. So where does Finest come into it?"
>
> "Finest is a networking organisation that brings them together to help to build business relationships, collaborate and bring business into the area. It works really well for that too!"
>
> "So you've got a room full of successful professional services organisations who are also part of a successful networking organisation, so why on earth

have they asked you to speak?" I'm hoping his question was one of incomprehension rather than incredulity!

"Hmm, good question. I suppose it's because they are all based locally and that Stoke City are now in the Premier League and that I work for the club."

"So what do you think they probably really want you to talk about?"

"I suppose, probably some footballing stories and behind the scenes gossip."

"Then why don't you talk about that then?!?"

And he did, and it was a great speech!

The reason I'm quoting this as an example is so I can highlight the subtle messages that Tony inferred in his opening, in what appeared to be just a simple story.

Let's read between the lines:

- I'm going to start by stating that I spent some time working out what to say to you today – I've not just thrown my speech together.
- Then I'm going to show that I know who my audience is.
- Then I'm going to compliment my audience on being successful businesses.
- Then I'm going to speak positively about the organisation that invited me to speak.
- And I'll finish by showing that I really understand my audience in recognising what the real reason probably is why they have actually invited me, so I'll talk about that.

By the end of his Attention Grabber the audience felt great (because of all of those positive strokes) and were really looking forward to hearing those stories!

Example: A linked Attention Grabber and Attention Focuser

Steph Talbot, from BespokeFD, is an independent Financial Director and I had the pleasure of working with her on a spotlight presentation that she needed to do for her networking group.

Steph was frustrated by some other accountants as they very often just gave their clients their accounts and then did nothing more with respect to then using that information for something useful. In her eyes, Steph's USP is that she takes the accounting data and does then actually do something with it. She turns it into management information so that her clients can then make business decisions to make a positive difference to their business.

That was her core message.

So this was her Attention Grabber:

> I would like to introduce you to my grandson Loui.
>
> (She put up a picture of him – he was about 5, the audience thought he was cute!)
>
> Loui is a wonderful grandson and has a very inquisitive mind. He always wants to know what's next and he does this by asking a very simple question: And?
>
> (A speech bubble appears on the screen from Loui's mouth with "And?" in it)
>
> Let me give you an example.
>
> We are going to the zoo tomorrow Loui.
> Cool! And?
>
> Well there will be lions and tigers.
>
> Great! And?
>
> There will probably be snakes and creepy-crawlies too.
>
> Ooooo. And?
>
> And lots of other animals.
>
> Excellent. And?
>
> Well we'll probably have a burger for lunch.
>
> Yummy. And?
>
> Maybe an ice cream in the afternoon.
>
> Brill! And?
>
> You get the idea! I love him to bits but he always wants more.
>
> So why am I telling you this?
>
> Well I'll come back to that a bit later…

So at that point the audience was not only in a good mood because of the picture and the story to which many of her audience could relate as they were also parents or grandparents, the audience was also intrigued and curious about what Steph was going to say and where her grandson fitted into that.

Steph then went on to deliver her presentation covering what she did, how she was different and what she could do for her audience, i.e. take their accounting data, turn it into management information so that they could then make business decisions, i.e. what some other accountants didn't do.

To emphasise that core message, her Attention Focuser was simply this:

> *So the next time your accountant gives you your accounts, be like my grandson Loui.*
>
> *Ask them "And?".*
>
> *If they don't have a good answer to that question, then come and see me, because I do!*

This was a very clear call to action, a very clear core message that was easy to remember due to the story about her grandson.

Even Larry with his very full bladder could remember that!

Example: The whole Content Pie Sandwich in action

Sonia Clewlow is the owner of Purple Cow Training, a training company based in Staffordshire specialising in Health & Safety. Due to her company's national reputation, Sonia was asked to tender for some of the Health & Safety requirements for John Lewis, one of the UK's leading retailers. As part of that tendering process, Sonia needed to do a presentation.

Sonia's core message was this: we know what we're doing, we've done it before for large organisations, we can do it well for you too.

So this is what her Content Pie Sandwich looked like:

> ***(Top Bit of Butter)***
>
> *Hi.*
>
> *I'm Sonia Clewlow and I'm the owner of Purple Cow Training.*
>
> *Thank you for the opportunity to talk with you here today.*
>
> ***(Attention Grabber)***
>
> *I'd like to start off by showing you a quote.*

(Sonia then put up a slide and gave her audience the time to read it. The quote was from David, the CEO of a large, well-known, highly successful UK company, and it basically said that they had been using Purple Cow Training for a number of years, that they were very happy with Purple Cow Training as their training provider and that they would continue to use them in the future.)

As you can see, David believes that we have been doing a good job for his company for a number of years.

My goal here today, is to show you how we could do the same for you.

(Introduction)

To do that, I'm going to start by giving you a quick overview of our company.

Then I'll go into more detail about what we see your training requirements as being.

And I'll finish off by taking you through how we can meet those training needs for you.

(Sub-topic 1)

So who are we?

(Sonia gave a brief history and capability summary of Purple Cow Training.)

So that's a bit about us.

(Sub-topic 2)

I'd like to now talk about what we see your training requirements as being.

(Sonia went into depth on her analysis of their training requirements)

Those are your requirements as we see them.

(Sub-topic 3)

This is how we can meet those needs for you.

(Sonia painted the picture of how Purple Cow Training could meet those needs)

And that's how we'd do it!

(Summary)

So I've told you a bit about us as a company, what we see your training requirements as being and how we can meet those needs for you.

(Attention Focuser)

(Sonia put the quote slide up again).

I'd like to now finish by coming back to David's quote.

We've looked after his company's training requirements for years.

I strongly believe that we can do the same for you too!

(Bottom Bit of Butter)

Thank you for the opportunity of presenting to you here today .

From the top to the bottom, it was a clear message that Sonia was putting across: we've done it for other businesses like you so we can do it for you too!

The ABC for Short Videos

For helping you to create short videos that will hit their mark and get watched.

The **ABC for Short Videos** is a simple three-step framework for approaching the creation of a short video. By short, I mean about three minutes or less. For videos longer than this the **Content Pie Sandwich** Framework could be used.

Like the **Content Pie Sandwich**, this framework helps with the **Structure** step in the **PRESENTER** Framework. Therefore all of the other steps in that framework are equally valid here for a short video as they are for a longer presentation. For example, your video still needs to have a defined purpose, you need to know who the intended recipients are etc.

I would therefore encourage you to still use the **PRESENTER** Framework even if it's only a short video that you are creating.

Online videos are becoming more and more popular as a means of presenting content to audiences. As this popularity grows, so does the physical number of videos out there and that means that for a video to actually be watched it needs to stand out from all of the other videos. This means that it's even more important for them to be interesting, understandable and memorable.

Let's look at each of the steps in turn.

ABC

Grab their **Attention**.

Start with something that will grab your viewer's attention and make them want to watch your video. It's exactly the same principle as the top outer crust in the **Content Pie Sandwich**.

In many ways, though, with the online world that we live in today it's even more important to do this. If you're anything like me and you want to find a video about something online you'll do the following:

1. go to your favourite video hosting platform
2. search for what you are looking for
3. choose one of the videos that looks interesting
4. start to watch it
5. within the first minute or two (maximum)
   - if it has grabbed your interest, continue to watch it
   - if it hasn't, select the next video
6. go to step 4

With so much choice and competition for your time as a viewer, videos almost become disposable items and so those videos that are interesting right from the start will get watched the most.

For your video to be one of those videos, it has to grab the viewer's attention and grab it quickly. You need to help them to understand what they will get out of watching your video, why the time taken to watch your video will be time well spent.

A**B**c

This is the main **Body** of your presentation.

This is where you provide your content.

This is where your main message is.

AB**C**

There are three options for the **C** step here.

One you will definitely use, the other two you might also use.

What you will definitely need to have is a **Conclusion**. Something that brings your video to a close, a quick summary perhaps.

Depending on the nature of the video there are two other options that you might like to add after your conclusion:

- a **Challenge**
- a **Call to action**

These are particularly useful if the purpose of your video is to get the viewer to do something for themselves, or for you.

It's the same principle as the bottom outer crust in the **Content Pie Sandwich**.

And in the online world your message needs to be really crystal clear so don't forget Larry…

I have created a blank template for you to use when you are creating your own videos using this framework for the structure. You can download that template from the Resources section of my website: www.intercog.co.uk.

Online Considerations

By its very nature, the whole of this framework pertains to the creation of online content.

Part 3

How to Deliver with Confidence

Audience-focused, message-centric, well-structured presentation created – check!

Presentation rehearsed and rehearsed – check!

Delivery aids created and present – check!

All you need to do now is to deliver your presentation with confidence. It's all you need to do…

It's also easier said than done!

However, thinking back to the **CAPS** Framework, your confidence will be building because you have been thinking about your **Audience** (**A**) and doing your **Preparation** (**P**).

This part of the book will focus more on the **Skills** (**S**) side of things, while still keeping one eye on the **Audience** (**A**) of course.

So I'll be covering:

- where to start
- what you can do
- what you'll need to do this
- and a final thought on how to avoid planting seeds of doubt with your audience

So in this part of the book I've got four frameworks for you, frameworks that together will help you to deliver your presentations with confidence.

The Confidence Cycle

For helping you to know where to start in being more confident when delivering your presentation.

There are lots of different theories about where to start when trying to be more confident when you are up there at the front of the room, presenting to your audience.

For me, the place to start is very simply to **know how to look like you are confident**.

If you look like you are confident, people will think that you are confident.

If people think that you are confident, they will treat you as if you are confident.

If they treat you as if you are confident, then that will make you feel more confident.

If you feel more confident, then you'll start to look even more confident.

And so the cycle continues – it's the Confidence Cycle!

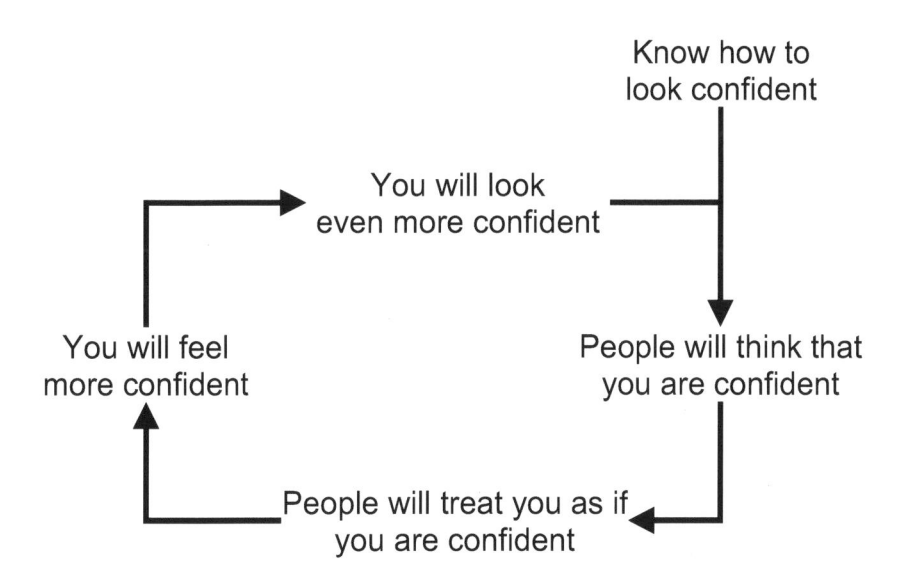

```
                              Know how to
                              look confident
                                   |
                                   v
        You will look
        even more confident
           ^                          |
           |                          v
    You will feel              People will think that
    more confident             you are confident
           ^                          |
           |                          v
           +— People will treat you as if —+
               you are confident
```

So the place to start your confidence building journey is to learn the tips, tricks and techniques about how to look like you are confident and the frameworks in this part of the book will help with that.

Before getting to the frameworks, however, there's a quick tangent to mention. If you make a mistake while you are presenting, you will know that it has happened as you know what you should have said or done. But will your audience know or realise that it has happened?

If it is not obvious that a mistake has been made, then don't draw attention to it by apologising or pointing it out. Keep your confident external demeanour and then adjust what happens next to compensate for the mistake. For example, if you meant to talk about A then B then C but for some reason started talking about C before B, then, as long as there is no obvious order, finish off C and then come back to B without mentioning that B should have come earlier. Nobody in the audience will know that you went ACB rather than ABC and so don't undermine the confidence they have in you by letting on and telling them.

Of course, if it was obvious that the order needed to be ABC or what happened was unmissable (like falling off the stage for example), then in those circumstances it's best to admit that it had happened and then carry on.

Online Considerations

The Confidence Cycle applies regardless of the mode of delivery.

The SPEAKER Framework

For helping you to exude confidence when presenting.

The **SPEAKER** Framework is a seven-part acronymic guide.

Each of the letters represents one tip, trick or technique to help you to look confident.

And if you look confident…

Let's examine each letter in turn.

SPEAKER

The first part of the **SPEAKER** Framework is a very simple thing and that is just to **Smile**.

Not a manic, nervous smile but a normal, natural smile.

Picture somebody with a nice natural smile on their face. What emotions could they potentially be feeling? Grab some paper and a pen and write some down…

Now review your list. I suspect on your list you will have things like:

- relaxed
- confident
- prepared
- knowledgeable
- content
- happy
- ready

That's because these are the sorts of emotions that you would naturally associate with somebody who's got a big smile on their face.

Now let's look at it from the other side. That person with the natural smile on their face, what emotions are they probably not feeling? What is it unlikely that they are feeling if they have a smile on their face?

Again, write a few of those down on your piece of paper.

On your list, you've probably got things like:

- nervous
- anxious
- scared
- unprepared
- sad
- sick

Surely nobody with a natural smile on their face would be feeling any of those emotions, would they?

And therein lies the secret!

When we see somebody smiling naturally we instinctively assume that those positive emotions apply, that they are happy, ready and knowledgeable. That they're confident. It doesn't compute within us that they could be feeling any of those negative emotions because if they were, they wouldn't be smiling. We just naturally assume that all of those positive emotions are being felt and none of the negative ones are.

That's what is so simple, and effective, about this technique.

But it gets better!

There are also physiological benefits to smiling. When you smile certain chemicals are released in your body which affect you by lowering your heart rate and blood pressure, helping you to feel more relaxed and working as an anti-depressant, i.e. a mood lifter.

In simple terms, smiling actually makes you feel better! And if you feel better on the inside, you'll look better on the outside which is, after all, all your audience can see, which links back to the **Confidence Cycle** I mentioned earlier.

So clearly it's a good idea to have a nice natural smile on your face but it's not always so easy, however, to bring a smile to your face when you need one.

When I ask people how they can conjure a smile when they need one, they normally say something along the lines of "Think happy thoughts!". Those thoughts could be people, places, memories or whatever – it's different from person to person.

The link here, though, is to the **Preparation (P)** in the **CAPS** Framework. As part of your preparation, work out what your "happy thoughts" are and then you can call on them when you need to. At the time of the presentation you don't want to be trying to work out what your "happy thoughts" are (while you're actually possibly stressed and nervous). You want to be actually thinking about them and smiling!

Internationally renowned professional speaker David Hyner always takes with him his "Feel Good Book". It contains pictures, awards, testimonials – all kind of things that make him happy, that make him proud of what he's done when he looks at them. It's his way of bringing a smile to his face, of helping himself to feel better.

So what would you put in yours? (And when are you going to create it and start using it?)

Smiling is also infectious. If you look at somebody who is smiling what's your natural response? To smile back!

You can use that as a technique to help you to smile when you're at the front of the room. Look for someone in the audience who is smiling and make eye contact with them. This will bring out your own smile.

You can also use this technique in reverse. Whilst smiling, look for someone in the audience who isn't smiling and make eye contact with them. This normally brings out a smile on their face too and then the chemicals go to work making them feel better. Do this with multiple audience members and you'll be helping them to feel better and therefore to be more receptive to your presentation.

Oh, and don't worry about those that don't smile back – perhaps their smile muscles don't work properly or perhaps they are smiling on the inside and just haven't told their face yet…

So the first step in looking confident is simply just to smile.

sPEAKER

The **P** in the **SPEAKER** Framework stands for this: **adopt good Posture (and breathing)**.

Clearly there are two parts to this so I'll start with the posture bit first.

Adopt Good Posture

Strong, upright posture simply exudes confidence. Think of the professions that you see standing with this upright position. People in the armed forces, the Police, politicians, royalty. Anybody whose job it is to exude an air of confidence will have this upright posture because it is a very confident way to stand. So if you're standing up straight, people think that you're confident.

Not only is good posture a key part of looking confident, it also links into some of the other parts of the **SPEAKER** Framework and helps to prevent things getting in the way of those, as I'll cover later.

So let's investigate what good posture is.

It's time for an activity!

> To help you to do this activity I have created a video that illustrates what needs to be done (and matches the textual description below). You can access that video in the Resources section of my website: www.intercog.co.uk

What I need you to do is to find a door and then close it. Stand close to the door with your back towards it. Position your feet about a shoulder's width apart. Keeping that separation, put your heels against the bottom of the door. Now put your buttocks against the door and rest your shoulder blades against the door. Let your arms drape naturally by your sides. Finally, hold your head nice and relaxed on top of your neck and shoulders.

How does it feel? Unnatural? Awkward?

It wouldn't be surprising if it did!

Admittedly, this is a slightly exaggerated position because you're standing with your back actually touching the door. So the next thing to do is to take half a pace forward. Now *imagine* that you have the door at your back. Put your feet a shoulder's width apart. Align your heels, buttocks and shoulder blades against your imaginary door. Drape your arms and relax your head.

How does it feel now?

Probably less unnatural or awkward and yet you are standing in exactly the same way. It was most likely the door that was making it feel more peculiar or odd. And talking of odd, your arms might feel a bit strange just hanging by your sides but there's a reason why they are there like that which I'll be back to in a moment.

The goal is therefore, whenever you are in front of an audience, you should adopt good posture as it's a great way to exude confidence.

There is a slight snag, however.

I'm suggesting that you have this good posture whenever you are in front of the audience but you don't want to be going through the motions of imagining your heels, buttocks and shoulder blades against the door and straightening yourself up in front of everybody else because you'll just look a bit weird, So clearly what you need to do is have that good posture by the time that you get to the front of the room.

And here's another snag.

You have to get from the door where you walk into the room to the front of the room from where you are going to speak. If you went through this straightening process as you made that journey then again you're going to look particularly odd and that's not a great first impression to make. Fortunately, you've just walked through a door...

So I've got another activity for you!

> To help you to do this activity I have created a video that illustrates what needs to be done (and matches the textual description below). You can access that video in the Resources section of my website: www.intercog.co.uk

Open the door that you used in the last activity and stand underneath its frame, i.e. halfway through the door. Adopt your good posture position as before.

Imagine that there is a piece of string hanging from the door frame and on the end of which there is a tennis ball. The length of the string is such that the tennis ball just rests ever so gently on top of your head.

Take a few paces away from the door, turn around and visualise the string and the tennis ball hanging from the frame. The goal here is to get the tennis ball to glance off the top of your head as you walk through the door. Of course, the only way you will be able to do this is if you have adopted your good posture position by the time you get to the door frame. (Jumping up and heading the ball football-style is not really an option!)

So as you approach the door frame you need to go through those mental steps of your heels and your buttocks and your shoulder blades straightening up nicely with your head being nicely relaxed on your shoulders so that by the time you get to the door frame you've got your great posture and the tennis ball glances off your head.

> *When I've used this activity on training courses, which I have done a lot, people are sometimes so focused on straightening up and glancing the tennis ball off the top of their head that they forget to swing their arms whilst they are walking. That looks very peculiar and unnatural and is definitely not the impression we were going for! So let your arms do their natural thing and swing like they would do normally.*
>
> *Also, for some unknown reason, some people think they have to glance the ball off their nose. Don't ask me why they think this! They looked even more odd than those with non-swinging arms. So keep your head nice and relaxed and let the tennis ball glance off the top of it.*
>
> *And finally, almost everybody who does this activity on the course walks in with a big smile on their face. Now where have you heard that before?*

If you adopt this mental strategy as you walk towards a door then you will enter the room with your good posture in place and look confident from the very moment you enter the room.

> **T**
>
> *This is a really easy technique to practise. Just think for a moment about how many times you walk through a door frame every day. I suspect that you will have got to at least twenty by the time you leave for work in the morning. If you consciously think about using this technique every time you walk through a door frame then in two or three days it will become a habit and you will naturally therefore enter every room in the future looking confident.*

Let's now come back to your arms when you are standing with your good posture. I talked earlier about letting your arms just hang loosely and naturally by your sides. It doesn't feel very natural at all and if you were to start talking your hands and arms would probably be itching to do stuff.

By having your arms naturally by your sides it will then encourage them to gesture and those gestures will help you to explain your story and help the audience to understand what it is you're saying. Having them by your sides allows them to do this. If your hands were in your pockets, or your arms were folded or behind your back, then that is going to get in the way of them doing what they want to do.

The other thing to consider here is the non-verbal message that your hands and arms are communicating. People with their hands in their pockets are often perceived as being insecure, not confident or disinterested. Folded arms can be seen as defensive whilst arms behind the back could be taken as overconfidence or pride. None of these are what you want to convey to your audience, especially if that's not how you are actually feeling.

Not having your hands in your pockets also stops you playing with whatever it is that you might have in your pockets and that could be a distraction for everyone!

Clearly, though, some speakers are not naturally big gesticulators and that's perfectly fine! For them, starting with their arms by their sides allows their hands to move into a naturally comfortable position, probably gently clasped in front of them, from where they can then gesture if needed.

The key point is that, however much you gesture, the good postural starting position allows you to do what you would naturally do and so you appear to be yourself. I'll come back to this point when I talk about the second **E** in this framework.

Let's now come back to the bit in brackets – breathing.

Breathing

Breathing is good, obviously!. But maximised, controlled breathing is even better.

Good posture maximizes the capacity of your lungs and increases the effectiveness of your breathing. The more air that you can get into your lungs the more oxygen goes into your blood stream. The more oxygen in your blood then the more oxygen that goes to your brain and this will help you to think more quickly and also more clearly. One of the other effects of having lots of oxygen in your blood is it actually slows your heart rate down and causes it to pump more strongly. This has the added bonus of making you feel more relaxed.

Compare that to someone who has not got their breathing under control. They might be struggling for breath, panting or talking in only short or partial sentences. You might also see their racing heartbeat in the veins on their neck. All in all, it's not a confident look!

If you've got your hands in your pockets or your arms folded in front of you or you're leaning on a podium or something else, then you are reducing the capacity for your lungs to take in air and therefore you're reducing your maximum breathing capability.

The other advantage of having lots of air in your lungs is that it gives you greater control when you are speaking. When you speak you breathe out as well and so the more air you have in your lungs, the longer that you can speak before needing to breathe in again. Not that I'm suggesting that you should ramble on and speak for as long as you can before running out of breath, more that it just gives you the flexibility then to choose when to stop talking and when to then take your next breath in. Also, if you need to speak more loudly you can do that more easily without appearing to strain. Similarly, you will have greater ability to vary your volume if you are breathing effectively.

spEaker

The first **E** in the **SPEAKER** Framework is all about **maintaining appropriate Eye contact**.

When you're having a conversation with someone, the best way to engage with that person is to look them in the eye as direct eye contact draws people into the conversation. The person that you are looking at feels like you are giving them your personal focus and that, at that moment, they have all of your attention.

It also takes a certain amount of confidence to look someone in the eye and those people that don't are, perhaps unfairly, labelled as sheepish, shy or unconfident. So again, similarly to what I talked about in the **Smile** section, simply looking people in the eye implies the confidence needed to do it and not doing it implies a lack of confidence.

Also, when you are chatting to somebody and they don't give you the level of eye contact that you would perhaps expect, your brain then starts to wonder why they are doing this. Are they distracted, not interested in you or more interested in someone else or perhaps trying to hide something? This also therefore works against them creating a positive, confident impression.

On the flip side, if somebody gives you too much eye contact, how does that make you feel? I'm guessing that the first word that popped into your head was "uncomfortable".

Again, your brain starts wondering why they are doing this. Are they being aggressive, avoiding looking at someone else or have you just got spinach stuck in your teeth? Whatever their reason, it again has a negative impact on how they come across.

So the key word here is *appropriate* – enough to engage them but not so much as to make them feel uncomfortable.

Turning from conversations to presentations, clearly there are more people that you are talking to but the principle still holds as appropriate eye contact is still a great way to help your audience to feel engaged.

If you have a relatively small audience, say up to about twelve people, then it is actually possible to spread your eye contact around them all. You can move around the room giving people eye contact, holding their gaze for a few seconds before moving onto the next person in turn. When doing this, it's important to move from side to side rather than going all the way around the room one way and then all the way around the other way and then doing it again (and again and again). Imagine drawing lines between the people that you look at consecutively and aim for as many crossovers in those lines as possible.

If you have more than about a dozen people then it's pretty much impossible to make individual eye contact with everybody in the audience. In this case, just split your audience up into groups. So if you've got, for example, fifty people in the audience, split them up into about eight or ten groups and then look at the middle of that group and work around the different groups in the room in the same way that you would for a smaller number of people. Each time you return to a group, look at a different person to bring in a bit of variation within the groups too.

If you are more than about fifteen feet away from your audience, if you look in the general direction of a group, it's very difficult for any one person in the group to know exactly who it is that you're looking at. So if you look at a group of four or five people then probably two or three of them think that you are actually looking at them directly and so that it's them with whom you are making eye contact, that it's with them that you are engaging.

As you work around the room and in this way, the whole audience will be engaged as they all have the perception that you are giving them the appropriate level of eye contact that they would expect and require.

To finish off these thoughts on eye contact, I have a question for you that might at first glance appear odd but there is, however, a point to it.

If the goal is to be maintaining appropriate eye contact with your audience while you are talking, then which way do you need to be facing while talking?

I can imagine your furrowed brows at this moment as surely the answer is obvious – towards your audience!

And it is the obvious, and only, answer. So why am I asking such a seemingly obvious, almost pointless, question?

Because, in practice, people don't always do it and, what's more, often don't realise that they're not doing it. Here are a few examples:

1. People reading, perhaps verbatim, from their notes and not looking up at the audience.
2. People talking to the projection screen/monitor.
3. People talking to a flip chart/whiteboard whilst drawing on it.

There are many more examples all of which share the same bad practice: talking whilst not looking at the audience. Fortunately, though, there are some simple fixes:

1. People reading, perhaps verbatim, from their notes and not looking up at the audience:
   - don't have too much detail on your delivery notes
   - get into the habit of stopping talking, glancing down then back up again, then restarting talking
   - use your slides as your cues instead of your notes
     - bear in mind Point 2 below though
   - be prepared and confident enough to not need any notes
2. People talking to the projection screen/monitor:
   - position your laptop/computer in front of you so you can look at that rather than the slides behind you
     - don't be afraid to rearrange the room/stage as required to allow for this
   - practise looking at your laptop, not at what's behind you
     - if you do happen to glance at the screen behind you, which is quite a natural thing to do, stop talking while you do so
3. People talking to a flip chart/whiteboard whilst drawing on it:
   - stop talking before turning to draw
   - don't talk whilst drawing
   - start talking again *only* when you are back facing your audience
   - use your turning as the cues to stop and start talking accordingly
   - remember that your audience will allow you time to draw whatever you need to draw, so you don't need to talk whilst doing it

It goes without saying that the better you know your presentation, the more you know what you're going to say, the less you'll need to refer to anything else and so the more you can concentrate on your audience and give them the appropriate level of eye contact.

SPE**A**KER

The **A** in the **SPEAKER** Framework is all about **making sure that you are Audible**.

If I were to ask people for a definition of what audible means, most of their answers would probably say that it's about needing to speak loudly enough so that people can hear you. And that is certainly part of what this **A** is all about.

The simple trick about volume is to talk loudly enough so that the person who is at the back of the room can hear you. If they can hear you, then so can everyone else. This is the approach to take even if you are using some sort of sound system. You still need to project your voice to that person at the back of the room. Technology helps with your projection – it doesn't do it all for you. Linking back to the **Posture** part of the **SPEAKER** Framework, your good posture helps with your breathing which in turn helps with your projection.

Audibility, though, is not just about people being able to hear you. It's also about them hearing what you are saying or, in other words, them being able to take in what you are saying and then understanding it. This links back to the goal of the **PRESENTER** Framework in that you're aiming for your presentation to be interesting, *understandable* and memorable.

Part of this is about speaking clearly, about annunciating well and not mumbling so your audience can accurately hear the words that you are saying.

Part of this, though, links back to the principle of taking the audience-focused approach that I have mentioned a number of times in this book. For your message to be clear, you need to use words and terms that are known to your audience. Having an understanding of your audience and what they know about what you are talking about will help you to choose those words appropriately.

Also, to help your audience to take in and understand what you are saying you also need to actually stop talking on occasion. You need to introduce appropriate gaps into your delivery.

If you think of the written word, it's broken up into sentences, paragraphs and chapters to help the reader to take in the text. The same applies when speaking and gaps should be used to provide the same help for your listeners to take in what you are saying. Using suitable gaps gives your audience the mental moment to take in what you've said. Talking and talking and talking without any gaps deprives your listeners of those moments to take in what you've said and so it will be harder for them to understand your message.

Gaps are also great for emphasising key points. If you want to make a key point…

…put a big gap in front of it!

It works like a pregnant pause and focuses the attention of your audience so they don't miss it.

And if it's a really, really important point…

…put a big gap in front of it…

…and after it, so there's plenty of time for it to sink in with your audience.

SPEA**K**ER

The **K** in the **SPEAKER** Framework is to **(remember that you) Know what you're talking about**.

As "*remember that you*" is in brackets, I'll come back to that later.

It's a fairly obvious thing to say but if you know what you're talking about then your presentation will go better than if you don't!

There are links here to earlier parts of this book:
- to the **CAPS** Framework where the **P** stood for **Preparation** - the more prepared you are, the more you will know what you are talking about and the more confident you will look and feel
- to the **YAT Triangle** - this is the "**Your perspective on the topic**" relationship
- to the **PRESENTER** Framework - being clear on your **Purpose**, understanding your **Recipients** and having a great **Structure** to your presentation will help you to come across like you know what you're talking about

Whilst it's important to consider all of those things, the key element here that actually gives the confidence boost is that bit in the brackets – to *remember that you* know what you're talking about.

Let me give you an example of what I mean.

Imagine that next week you have a Maths test and that passing this test is massively important to you. There are ten questions on the test and you need to get six answers correct in order to pass. Fortunately (and legitimately) you have today been given six of the questions from next week's test.

What are you going to do between now and the test next week?

You'll work out the answers to those six questions - obviously!

You're doing your preparation, or in other words, you're getting to know what you're talking about.

Now imagine yourself standing outside the examination room next week. How will you be feeling?

You'll probably be feeling a little nervous but you'll also be feeling more confident about taking the test because you know six of the answers already. In fact, if you take a conscious moment to stop and think about that fact, that you do know what you're talking about, you'll feel even more confident.

And that's the key.

Yes, you need to be prepared, but it's the taking of a moment to reflect on the fact that you do know what you're talking about that gives you that extra confidence boost.

> *I used to be part of the Staffordshire Marketing Academy and we ran live events twice a year for around a hundred people. It was part of my role to run an icebreaker energizer activity right at the start of the morning. Clearly this needed to go well or I'd severely scupper the mood and momentum of the event.*
>
> *So I would create the activity and test it on friends. I'd make sure all of the required materials were correctly set up on the tables in the room before everybody got there. I would create a script and practise, and practise, and practise that script so I knew exactly what I needed to say.*
>
> *The activity worked, the room was set up, my patter was ready. I was ready, I knew what I was talking about!*
>
> *On the morning of the event, everyone was in the foyer having breakfast. I was alone in the main room and everything was set up. I'd checked it – twice! As Denis Sidebottom, our wonderful compere, invited everyone into the main room, I went the opposite way into the foyer, which I now had to myself.*
>
> *And then I took a moment to consciously remember: activity – checked, tables – set up, patter – in my head!*
>
> *I'd then say to myself, "This is what I do!", turn round and stride into the room with a big natural smile on my face, glancing my virtual tennis ball off the top of my head on the way in of course!*

So yes it's important to be ready but it's also important to take a moment to remember that you are ready!

And don't forget that that also includes remembering that you know what you are going to say (the **N** in the **PRESENTER** Framework), that you know how you are going to deliver it (the final **E** in the **PRESENTER** Framework) and that you have rehearsed your presentation (the final **R** in the **PRESENTER** Framework).

SPEAK**E**R

The second **E** in the **SPEAKER** Framework is all about **Expressing yourself naturally**.

Before I talk about this point a bit more, I'd like to talk about your brain's "offness detector". OK, so that's not a proper name and I'm not going to offer any scientific evidence to back this point up but you will recognise the principle about which I'm talking!

We all have an "offness detector" in our brain and it's amazingly powerful. Think about somebody that you know really well. How long does it take you to realise that something's up with them, that they're not quite being themselves?

Milliseconds!

That's what your "offness detector" does. It detects "offness", variations and deviations from the norm.

Now the wonderful thing about this detector, though, is that it also works with people you don't know very well, or even at all. It's such a sensitive, finely tuned thing that it can actually tell if somebody you've never met before isn't quite being themselves, if something is up, for want of a better phrase. Don't ask me how your brain does it, it just does!

And then another wonderful bit of your brain kicks in. It's the part that tries to fill in gaps with reasons and explanations. Your brain starts to wonder why they aren't being themselves. Are they nervous, unprepared, unknowledgeable, ill, blasé, not bothered, lying, distracted? The probability is that you don't know or won't find out the reason but it doesn't really matter what the reason actually is. The damage has been done in that the "offness" your brain has detected has undermined that confidence that you have in them as a speaker. You are also being distracted from what they are saying because your brain is partially otherwise occupied, hypothesising why.

And this is why expressing yourself naturally is so important. If you are being yourself, the "offness detector" in your audience's brains won't go off. The gap-filling part of their brains will have nothing to do, their confidence in you won't be undermined and there won't be any unhelpful brain activity to interfere with what you are saying.

It's one of those reversal thinking things again. If you're being yourself, then you can't be nervous, unprepared, unknowledgeable, ill, blasé, not bothered, lying or distracted. So your audience assumes that you're the opposite: confident, ready, knowledgeable, well, sincere, bothered, truthful and focussed.

SPEAKE**R**

The final step in the **SPEAKER** Framework is to **Remember your Recipients**.

Yes, it all comes back to where you started your journey in thinking about your audience first!

So, remember that you've thought about your relationship with your audience and what they know about what you're talking about.

Remember that you've tailored your content and its wording so that it's understandable to them.

Remember that they are right there in front of you and that you're going to use the previous techniques to engage with them both individually and collectively.

Remembering (and using) all of these things will help each audience member to feel like the presentation has been created and delivered just for them and that will help with how it will be received.

So start by thinking about your audience and end by thinking about your audience. Doing that will make a huge difference to them, you and your presentations in the future.

Recap

Putting it all together, here's a summary of the **SPEAKER** Framework:

Smile
Adopt good **P**osture (and breathing)
Maintain appropriate **E**ye contact
Make sure you are **A**udible
(Remember you) **K**now what you are talking about
Express yourself naturally
Remember your **R**ecipients

Online Considerations

Let's look at each step in turn.

Smile

This all still applies.

Adopt good Posture (and breathing)

Many presenters stand up when delivering online and recording videos as it feels more familiar, comfortable and effective for them. If you do this too then all of the above is clearly still applicable.

If, however, you are sitting down when you present then the posture principles still hold but need to be adapted:

- set the height of your chair to be such that your shins are vertical, your feet are flat on the floor and your thighs are horizontal
- your buttocks should be at the rear of the seat with your back going straight up the back of the chair
- your arms should naturally come down so your hands are in your lap
- your head needs to be resting in a relaxed way on your shoulders
- and also:
    - avoid leaning on arm rests
    - avoid rocking backwards and forwards excessively
    - try not to spin around too much

As with the standing posture, the goal is to adopt a position that will help you to deliver and not get in the way of being able to do so. In the same way that there is some movement when you present standing up, there should be some movement when you present sitting down as well, although rolling around the floor on your chair is taking it too far...

And of course, adopting this posture whilst you are sitting down will also help with your breathing as well and any natural gestures that you might make.

Regardless of whether you are standing or sitting, though, ensure that your camera is at eye level. If it's too low, your audience will be looking up your nose and it will also increase the number of chins that you appear to have – neither of these are desirable! If it's too high, you will look aloof and get a bad neck as well. You need to be resting your head in a relaxed and even way whilst looking directly into the camera.

Maintain appropriate Eye contact

More and more presentations these days are being delivered online to a live audience or being recorded and watched later. Even in these situations where it's not a physically in-person situation, appropriate eye contact is still important but the mechanics are slightly different.

For a recorded presentation, it's fairly straightforward. Look at the camera!

(You will find that you will naturally glance away from the camera in the same way as you would do if you were talking to a single person.)

When the video is watched back, it will feel to the viewer like they are being looked at and communicated with directly and that's a good thing.

For a live, but online, presentation, the advice is still the same. Look at the camera!

However, simple though that may seem to do, in practice, it's not always that straightforward. In a live, online environment where you can see the faces of your audience, your eyes will be drawn to those faces. It's the natural thing to do as you will feel like you are looking at your audience.

The snag is that you are not. If you are looking at the faces on your screen, you are looking at your screen, not looking at your camera. If you are not looking at your camera, then it will look to your audience as if you are looking at something else and not them. That will have a detrimental effect on your audience in exactly the same way as if you were physically in the room in front of them and not looking at them..

There are, however, a number of things that you can do to help you to look at the camera more.

Simple though it may seem, the first approach is just to get into the habit of looking at your camera and not the faces on your screen. It will feel odd to you because it will feel like you are not looking at your audience. However, to your audience, the people who are most important of course, it will feel like you are looking at them.

Because you are not looking at those faces, you may miss out on some visual clues from your audience but the more that you practise looking at the camera, the more that you will learn to pick up those clues with your peripheral vision. This is, in effect, what happens in reality when you are in the same room anyway.

The second approach is to move the faces on the screen as close to your camera as possible to reduce the feeling of distance between where you need to be looking and your audience looking back. For laptops, iPads etc., this normally means moving the windows to be just below your camera.

Another alternative is to buy a separate camera and use that. Often this extra camera is placed on top of the monitor/screen and so again it's a case of moving the windows on the screen to be just below that camera. It could also be positioned on a tripod in front of your screen so that the faces are behind it. It would almost feel then as if you are looking through your camera to your audience, although the camera will obscure their faces slightly.

Whichever approach you take, however, as with most things to do with presenting, practice makes better!

When I was talking about online considerations for the delivery aids that you could make for yourself I mentioned potentially having extra information on or around your screen or, indeed, having multiple screens. Whilst this is a valid approach, the obvious is worth stating that when you are looking at the extra information you are not looking at your camera and therefore not looking at your audience, which is not ideal. The only exception to this is if you can cunningly position that extra information so that it is behind your camera so you are effectively looking at both at the same time. For example, some presenters put things on the wall or a flip chart behind their monitor so it's still in view whilst looking at the camera.

Make sure you are Audible

If you are presenting online, you will be using a microphone.

The first thing to consider is which microphone to use. Options here include:

- the one that is built into your video device, e.g. camera, camcorder, phone
- a separate microphone that might be:
  - placed on your desk
  - held in a stand
  - clipped onto you

When choosing which to use bear in mind how far you are from the microphone, how much you move around and how much you move your head. In general, the closer your microphone is, and stays, to your mouth the better.

That being said, higher quality microphones can overcome distances and direction issues and wireless options can be used to overcome issues with wires.

Fortunately, you can experiment with different options and record and watch back those experiments to help you to choose what the best solution is for you. What you are aiming for is adequate volume and high clarity of sound. Different microphones could also be used for different occasions.

Everything else like annunciation, not mumbling, using audience-understandable terminology and using gaps well all clearly still apply to online delivery.

(Remember you) Know what you are talking about

This still applies and also extends to "know how to use the technology" and then, of course, remembering that you do know how to use it!

Express yourself naturally

30%.

Apparently that's the quoted figure as to how much energy is "lost down a camera" when you present. So to be you, the real you, you will need to give more energy to an online delivery than you would to an in-person one.

But still be you...

> **T** *Many people routinely talk to a camera as part of their jobs. Examples are news readers, reporters, documentary makers etc. A best practice that is common amongst them is to imagine that they are talking to a single person, rather than a larger audience, and that the conversation is only with them. They tend to choose someone they know well like a partner or best friend. They feel like they are talking through the lens, not to the lens. This approach helps them to come across more personably, to be more like their natural self.*

Remember your Recipients

Whether they are sitting there in front of you or off somewhere in cyberspace, they are still your recipients, your audience.

Remember that and them!

Be Environmentally Aware

For making sure everything you need to present well is present.

Imagine yourself delivering your presentation, in person, in front of your audience.

How would you describe that picture?

Pick out some details:

- Where are you standing?
- What technology are you using?
- Where is it placed relative to you?
- Where is your presentation being projected?
- What sound system is being used?
- Where are your audience?
- What are you wearing?
- Where is your glass of water?
- What delivery aids are you using and where are they?
- What have you taken as "backups" just in case things go wrong?

If you imagine the presentation in advance and the associated environment in which it is delivered you can then work out what's needed for it to go well. You can then ensure that this happens.

Things to think about, though:

- some aspects of the environment are under your control and so it's your responsibility to ensure that they happen
- other aspects of the environment are not under your control but it's still your responsibility to:
  - work out what they are
  - liaise with whoever is required to confirm that they will be done
  - avoid any issues that might arise because of incorrect assumptions
- if you are finding it hard to pick out some of the details above, do something to rectify that, e.g.:
  - if you don't know what the venue is like, go and pay it a visit
  - if you don't know if there's a sound system, contact the hosts and find out

The other thing to remember is that you have scope to request that adjustments are made to the delivery environment. Many presenters mistakenly believe that they have to deliver in the environment they are given but this is not necessarily the case. Many venues will work with you to tailor the environment to suit your needs. Admittedly, this isn't true in all cases but if you don't enquire you won't find out if it can be done.

The one final thing to say on this is similar to something I have said before. If you are aware of your environment, of what you need and have ensured that it is set up accordingly, then take a moment to reflect on that as you prepare to deliver your presentation. By reflecting in this way it will help you to feel more confident when you do then deliver your presentation.

> **T** *Don't let a cable trip you up! To be as safe as possible I take a VGA lead, two HDMI cables, an HDMI extender and an HDMI to VGA converter just in case the venue doesn't have the right cable, an old style projector or there's a long distance between where my laptop will be and the projector's input panel. Better safe than sorry...*

Online Considerations

Imagine yourself delivering your presentation but this time doing it online.

How is that picture different to the one above?

Which details are different and which are the same?

The biggest difference is that you are responsible for more of the environment as you will be providing much more of the technology. You'll therefore need to have that in place, have tested it before-hand and be able to use it properly. (I've touched on these aspects in various places earlier in the book)

The other difference is that you are also responsible for the environment around you, as opposed to the venue as before. So you need to consider:

- your lighting
  - it needs to be light enough
  - the light needs to be even across you
  - the light needs to be in front of you
    - avoid having light coming from behind you
- what is behind you in the background
  - make sure it's tidy and not distracting
  - make sure there are not passing distractions in the background
  - potentially use a backdrop
  - potentially use a virtual background
- background noise
  - make sure there isn't any
  - let others in your house/office know you are presenting and are needing a quiet environment
- standing vs sitting

- there's no reason why you can't be standing up whilst presenting online to mimic how you would have been presenting if you were doing it in person
- similarly, it's also possible to deliver effectively while sitting down
- the choice is yours but whichever choice you make you need to set up your environment around that choice, considering therefore, for example:
  - camera positioning
  - microphone choice and positioning
  - lighting
  - your chair (comfort, movement capability, non-squeakiness)
  - etc.

> *I have two environments set up in my home office for online delivery. One is for presenting/recording and one is for delivering online training/facilitation. You can find a video of how they are set up in the Resources section of my website: www.intercog.co.uk*

There are a few other things that are peculiar to delivering online:

- you still need to dress the part but avoid busy or checked patterns as they might cause interference through the camera
  - also beware of interfering with a virtual background if you are using one as that can lead to some very weird and undesirable effects!
- it may be possible for the technology to allow you to provide an "offline image" that is displayed when your video is turned off
  - this is more personal than just your name being displayed
  - choose your image wisely!
- unlike being there in person at a venue, you have total control of when your audience can see you so choose when to turn your video on and off so the audience only sees you at your best

With all of the above, though, what remains the same is that it is still your responsibility for ensuring that your environment is how it needs to be for your presentation.

Oh, and then taking a moment to reflect on the fact that you're all set up and good to go!

Don't Hope, Do!

For helping you to avoid planting seeds of doubt with your audience.

I have a problem with hope!

Not all hope in general, just specific, unwarranted hope that speakers sometimes offer to their audience.

Sometimes it's at the start of the presentation:

- Hopefully today…
- I'm hoping that by the end of this presentation…
- I hope that you will enjoy this talk…

And sometimes it's at the end:

- Hopefully that was useful for you.
- I'm hoping that you got something out of today.
- I hope you enjoyed my talk.

Merely the use of the word "hope" (or its derivatives) at the beginning of a presentation introduces a possible seed of doubt for your audience that they won't get things out of it, that they won't enjoy it, that it won't meet their expectations.

Saying "hope" at the end is akin to admitting that there is a possibility that the presentation hasn't gone as well as it could have done. What's more, you're airing that possibility for all to hear.

Now I know what you might be thinking on that one – your presentation might not have gone down as well as it could have done and you might be right!

But there's no need to share that thought in public by explicitly hoping out loud…

Very simply, if you have a significant measure of control over the outcome of something, don't verbalise a hope that it will happen, or has happened. Phrase things in the positive:

- Today I'm going to share with you…
- By the end of this session you will be able to…
- Today I covered…

So don't hope, do!

T *I'm no psychologist but I suspect that the word hope is a subconscious leaking of an internal lack of confidence into the external words that you are saying. It is therefore akin to other displacement activities that manifest nervousness externally for your audience to see and that goes against the goal of looking confident.*

It's such a natural thing to do that speakers do it regularly, often without realising that they are doing it. Maybe you do too! So next time you see a presentation, or even the next time you deliver one, keep an ear out for unwarranted hope.

Online Considerations

Don't hope online, do online!

Further Information

The "*Interact better. Achieve more.*" Series

This is the first title in the "***Interact** better. **Achieve** more.*" series.

The other titles in the series are:
- How to be Better at Networking - In Person and Online
- How to be Better at Communicating - In Person and Online

How to be Better at Networking - In Person and Online

Do any of these scenarios sound familiar:

- The thought of going networking fills you with dread. If only you had the courage to go along it might be good for you and your business.
- You have to go networking but hate every minute of it. You wish you could find a way of enjoying it more.
- It's great to catch up with people you know at these networking events. You know you should really start to chat to people you don't know but don't have the confidence to do that.
- Whilst networking, you never quite know what to say or how to say it. It would be really nice if you could let people know what you and your company do in a way that they would find useful.
- You're attending lots of networking events and making many new connections. Weirdly though, nothing seems to be coming out of it and you are wondering why.
- You've heard people talk about "networking online" but don't have much idea of how to do that, even though it sounds like a good idea.
- Your online networking activities are not as productive as your face-to-face ones. What techniques can you take from your in-person networking to your online networking to improve that situation?

These are all examples of where people are not achieving what they would like to when they are networking. There are many more examples like this and maybe you have your own variation on the above too.

In all of these cases, though, what's stopping people achieving what they want is actually very easy to identify – they don't know ***how*** to be a better networker.

So this book will give you that knowledge, the knowledge of how to be a better networker, together with the associated skills to do it. When you put that knowledge and those skills into practice, not only will you become a better networker, you will also become a more confident networker as well.

And by being a better networker with greater confidence, you will achieve whatever it is that you want to achieve.

With the ever-increasing use of technology in business, this book also includes considerations for networking online/remotely.

How to be Better at Communicating - In Person and Online

Do any of these scenarios sound familiar:

- Other people just don't seem to get what you're saying, even though it's perfectly clear in your own head.
- You don't understand the points that others are trying to make – life would be so much easier if you did.
- You thought you had said one thing and they thought you'd said something else (or vice versa) – it didn't end well…
- You spend way too much time in meetings because they just go on and on, they don't really achieve much or take ages to achieve anything at all
- You never quite know what the best way is to give somebody feedback in a way that will be well received and properly appreciated.
- Interviews are unnecessarily stressful and unsuccessful, either for the interviewee, the interviewer or both.
- People stop communicating because they find it "hard" or simply just not worth the effort.

Being able to communicate effectively is a core skill and is vital for achieving what you would like to achieve. Unfortunately, it's not always as straightforward as it might appear and less than effective communication can lead to a wide variety of undesirable results (like those above).

The foundation of being able to communicate effectively is a core knowledge set that is applicable to all occasions when communication is needed. On top of this foundation is specific knowledge that is required for particular occasions, e.g. for running meetings, giving feedback or being interviewed etc.

This book provides a set of frameworks for both the foundation and specific knowledge that is required to communicate effectively. In essence, it will give you the knowledge and skills for *how* to be a better communicator.

When you put that knowledge and those skills into practice, not only will you become a better communicator, you will also become more confident as a result.

By being a better communicator with greater confidence, you will therefore achieve whatever it is that you want to achieve.

And as with all of the titles in this series, with the ever-increasing use of technology in business, this book also includes considerations for communicating online/remotely.

About the Author

Mike's background is training. Mike delivered his first training session in 1989 and since then has delivered hundreds of sessions to thousands of people in over a dozen countries on three continents.

With audience sizes ranging from dedicated one-on-one training up to hundreds at international conferences, it's fair to say that Mike has helped a lot of people to learn a lot of stuff over the years!

Mike specifically started to help people to be better at presenting in the late 1990s not only through training sessions but also via one-to-one coaching. Mike's common-sense and insightful approach is highly effective for those with whom he works and he is a proven catalyst for helping people to be more effective, more confident presenters.

Complementing his training capabilities, Mike is also a skilled event designer and facilitator. All of Mike's events are entertaining and interactive, ranging from social activities like quizzes through to large scale networking events which he delivers for a number of local businesses and organisations, including a number of Chambers of Commerce.

With all of the wide variety of things that he does, Mike's professional goal is to help people to interact better and achieve more.

Mike can be contacted via his website at www.intercog.co.uk.